To my parents and to all my friends from Franklin High —
this book is for you.

Franklin:

From Puritan Precinct to 21st Century 'Edge City'

Eamon McCarthy Earls

Acknowledgements

The completion of this book would have been impossible without the generous contributions of a number of different individuals and organizations. The author wishes to thank the Franklin Historical Commission for their outstanding work to promote Franklin history, and tremendous contribution images, documents and encouragement, as well as the Franklin Public Library, E. Ross Anderson Library at Dean College, Franklin High School Library, and the Medway Public Library. In addition, several individuals deserve special thanks for their remarkable contributions, insights, and long term involvement with the Franklin community—Howard and Santina Crawford, the Compton family, and Ms. Vicki Buchanio of the Franklin Public Library.

Table of Contents

Maps and Illustrated Sections

Introduction

The story of Franklin, Massachusetts is a story of irrepressible change and growth. Our town has its beginnings as a precinct of Wrentham--as an autonomous, religious community. The roots of settlement go back centuries earlier, but the foundation of the precinct laid the ground for the Town of Franklin that came into being in 1778. The new town took its name from the famed American statesman and scientist, Benjamin Franklin, who granted the new municipal government books to establish what was in fact the nation's first public library.

For the next century, Franklin developed slowly from the hamlet that it was, into the town that it claimed to be. Horace Mann was born, and set off on a course to change the future of education in America. However, for the vast majority of Franklinites, life was carried on at a more earthly pace, regulated by the passing of the seasons, the demand for laborers at the mills, and the train schedules when the railroad arrived in the 1840s.

Franklin became a town, in a truer sense, starting in the 1870s and 1880s, with the expansion of railroads and industry, and the diversification of religious, social and political communities (the first Roman Catholics did not even move to Franklin until the 1840s, and not until the 1870s did they arrive in large numbers) and the arrival of trolleys. The advent of the 20th century saw many advances for the town--as everything from roads to community health improved. The new century also brought new challenges, such as resource shortages, horrible weather, a murderous influenza epidemic, and two world wars.

Only after World War II did Franklin begin to change its stripes. Fast growth, new money, and a new highway turned Franklin into a developers' paradise with two railroad stations, two highway interchanges (on the new Interstate-495, constructed in 1965), and plenty of farm land on which to build new neighborhoods. As the pace of development picked up in the 1980s, more and more commuters discovered the suburban charms of Franklin; new homes, shopping malls, and office parks beckoned. Today, Franklin stands as an example of what journalist Joel Garreau dubbed an 'edge city,' in his 1991 book, *Edge City: Life on the New Frontier*. Edge city is unlike any city from the past. It is a low-density urban area with a profusion of shops, businesses, houses, and entertainment outside a traditional urban center.

Franklin has been many things throughout its existence, but gradual changes have transformed the community from a rural precinct to an expanding, evolving, edge city. --*Eamon McCarthy Earls, 2012*

Part I:
Settlement & Incorporation

Wrentham and Franklin.

Reproduced on a uniform scale of 720 roads per inch from the old maps of Wrentham (1735) and Franklin

This early map of Franklin, dating from the 1790s, shows the main mills, and the town center as well as surrounding towns such as Wrentham, Medway, Attleborough, and the once very large town of Dorchester.

Chapter 1:

The First Tenants

...the extent of settlement at Beaver Pond may have been even greater than archaeologists guessed...

At the end of the last ice age, the region that we now know as New England shook itself free from its imprisonment in ice. For tens of thousands of years, wave after wave of ice crept down from the Arctic, covering modern day New England and New York with glaciers as much as a mile thick. The frigid climate was slow to change, but as temperatures began to rise the ice began to retreat.

Roughly 10,000 years ago, the last of the ice sheets melted away, leaving an exposed, open landscape that is hard to picture. From horizon to horizon stretched a gravel and boulder strewn terrain with only low hills to break the monotony. In fact, for a long time the land that we now know as Franklin was partly submerged thanks to glacial melt-water. Near Bellingham, the water was as much as 60 feet deep turning hills into islands.

With each passing year, as temperatures crept slowly higher, ice dams melted, allowing trapped melt-water to drain away into rivers and marshes. Mosses, then shrubs and trees began to grow again, reclaiming the land from gravel.

At around the same time, the first people were making their move into the region. Early Indians left more questions than answers; questions that archaeologists at the Robbins Museum in Middleboro have been trying to answer for decades. Finding answers can be difficult, especially since many sites where Native Americans lived are at ponds, areas cleared to make way for houses and beaches.

However, years of hard work have paid off, so that we do know some things about Indian life before colonization. Early Indians lived a simple and largely unchanging hunter-gatherer life style for about 9,000 years, using stone tools to hunt and prepare food.

Around 2,000 years ago, things changed again. Indians with an aptitude for farming set up shop, planting corn, squash and beans to supplement old favorites like fish and venison.

These were significant advances, but for Native American settlers in this area, life was still far from easy. Wild animals were plentiful in the forests, and fish were readily available in streams and ponds, but in order to catch any of these fast moving foods, stone tools were needed. Not all rocks were very good for "napping"--chipping away shards to create tools--and even getting raw materials was a painful process. According to the Robbins Museum, one of the main sources of local rock was a small quarry in present day Cumberland, Rhode Island. Native American 'miners' worked painstakingly to extract chunks of soapstone to make simple pots for storing and cooking food. With only wood and sand to dig with, one can imagine how tedious this work must have been. Using sand as an abrasive, and sticks to rub it in, these miners slowly extracted rock from the hillside to sand down further into pots.

Indian arrowheads hint at settlement, or at least hunting, centuries ago, but the full extent of settlement has long remained unclear. During the 1950s, an archaeologist named Stephen Keighley began to dig at the Eagle Head Dam in Wrentham (at Lake Pearl). His discoveries were surprising. He uncovered as many as 50 Indian hearths-- simple stone fire pits-- indicating a large, long term Indian settlement. In Keighley's view, these fire pits were just the beginning. He believed that many more had been covered over when the dam was built.

Keighley's work showed that settlements had existed around Lake Pearl, but it was not until the 1960s, that anybody bothered to look in Franklin. Ponds were often sites of Native American settlement; great sources of both fresh water and fish. Beaver Pond was no different. One archaeologist made a brief visit to Beaver Pond, and began to uncover artifacts almost immediately. Most strikingly, he discovered several pestles for grinding grain, with strange (and never before seen) lightning shaped markings chiseled into them.

In fact, the extent of settlement at Beaver Pond may have been even greater than archaeologists guessed. During the 1970s, when roadwork began on Pond Street, the town looked for a nearby source of sand to raise the road. They found an ample supply at the sandy hill alongside the pond. Hauling off the sand to fill in Pond Street created space for the new public swimming area known as Chilson Beach, but it also revealed signs of Indian settlement. At least two hearths were discovered, very similar to the ones at Lake Pearl. Unfortunately, even though some workers tried to contact the state archaeologist, others were in a hurry to get the job done and bulldozed the hearths along with any other Indian relics in the area. A subsequent expansion of the beach parking lot in the early 2000s further disrupted the area, wiping out what may be the last traces of Indian settlement at the site.

Because of this unfortunate development, we will never know much about the Indians who settled at Beaver Pond. However, it is thought provoking to remember that Native Americans inhabited this area for thousands of years, before Franklin's history was first recorded.

Chapter 2:

The New Settlers

...Settlers in Wrentham could see the writing on the wall. The town and its inhabitants might not survive an attack...

In 1630, Puritan ships anchored for the first time off of Massachusetts, establishing the Massachusetts Bay Colony by royal charter. Some of the first and most significant settlements were set up at Salem, Charlestown, and Boston, where good harbors offered an escape route if everything did not go as planned. With thousands of new arrivals pouring into the region, new settlements further inland were soon created.

With the exception of Boston itself, most of the settlements were to the north and west of the winding Charles River. Amongst those north of the river, were settlements such as Newtowne (modern day Cambridge), Concord, and Watertown. However, it was not long before settlers began to populate the region both south and east of the Charles River, filling in the gap in European settlement between Massachusetts Bay and Plymouth (at the time a separate colony).

In 1635, a new settlement was added to the books of the General Court. Contentment, the new 'plantation,' covered about 200 square miles of southeastern Massachusetts, land formerly controlled "on paper" by Newtowne. The plantation covered almost all of modern day Norfolk County, from the Charles River, south to modern day Attleboro.

Initially only a few hundred settlers moved to Contentment's center (now Dedham), building simple wooden houses and planting farms. The first act of the settlers after building homes was changing renaming the town Dedham, after a community in Britain.

The new town's enormous land area was only one of its attractions. The General Court granted the community a tax break and opened all swamps for woodcutting. With the exception of the town center, all land was considered 'common,' communally owned and open to all. Other tracts of land were owned by Indian tribes, and were not open for settlement until bought by the Europeans.

Dedham center was built around a muddy, dirt road, with houses and simple thatched roof huts on either side. Each house lot included 12 acres of privately owned land, with common land in back. About 90 houses stood in Dedham in the mid-1600s; one was used part time as a school house and another as an inn. In back of the pastures and cow commons, began a wall of swamps and forests. Southern New England was still populated with wolves that preyed on the settlers' sheep. Bounties for wolf scalps were high, and farmers would kill as many as possible to protect their livestock.

Thatch roofs are difficult to maintain, and settlers frequently ventured into nearby marshes and swamps, armed with scythes, to cut reeds for roofing and hay for livestock. As the 1660s came around, some community members were beginning to get restless, and rumors circulated of valuable metals (such as copper) in the large meadowlands to the west. The meadows and swamps along the Charles River and its tributaries (in current day Medfield, Sherborn, Norfolk, Franklin, and Medway) were already familiar to settlers, from annual reed cutting expeditions. As the rumors mounted interest in western Dedham grew.

The selectmen of the settlement appointed a cadre of four men to investigate extravagant claims about the western parts of the plantation. Leaving Dedham behind, the expeditionaries traveled inland by canoe. Although their findings are unknown, there was some substance to their belief in metal deposits. Occasional copper nuggets turned up, and bog iron was available in virtually every swamp.*

After the initial scouting, a group of Dedham citizens chose to pull up stakes in the town center and establish a new plantation in the west. The town arranged for subdivision of the land into a six hundred acre settlement, and the appointment of church officers, before turning its attention to the creation of roads and building a meeting house. Even before the settlers left, concerns about Indian attack surfaced. The settlers feared that their small numbers would be incapable of withstanding an Indian assault, and the plans for settlement were almost called off.

Although the Puritans were at peace with the major Native American tribes in southeastern Massachusetts—the Narragansetts and the Wampanoags—it was a shaky peace at best. Outside of the few European settlements in the Massachusetts Bay Colony, Plymouth Colony, and Rhode Island, sachems (Native American leaders) held sway over huge areas of land, even though they were much fewer in number than their European counterparts. Both of the main eastern tribes traded extensively with the English, but on a day to day basis, the citizens of Dedham dealt with members of the powerful Wampanoag Confederacy based at Mt. Hope, in present day Bristol, Rhode Island.

At the time that Dedham was setting up a western settlement, Metacom---better known as King Philip—succeeded his father,

*Bog iron typically forms by chemical accumulation of iron in acid swamps. Southern New England had significant bog iron reserves that were mined by early settlers, and melted down to make tools and utensils.

Massasoit, as leader of the Wampanoags. In 1662, when King Philip became the tribe's leader, the entire Confederacy was feeling the squeeze of European settlers. Colonists were continually pressuring the Indians into more land concessions, marketing guns and alcohol, or attempting to convert members of the tribe to Christianity. Compounding these problems, Indian villagers were continually falling ill with exotic European diseases such as measles and smallpox, as the food supply shrank with well-armed Europeans hunting down most local game. By the 1670s, King Philip was getting fed up with the aggressive behavior of the Europeans.

Even as trouble brewed with the Wampanoags, settlers from Dedham had finalized their plantation and settled the land near Lake Pearl. The new community was known as Wollomonopoag (present day Wrentham). Although it was far from Dedham center it remained subservient to the wider Dedham government. Wollomonopoag was smaller than Dedham, but had many advantages. River meadows were close by, saving home builders the trouble of trekking in search of reeds, and the wet fertile soil was well suited for grazing livestock and supporting fields of corn and rye to feed the first families.

Within a few years of settlement 34 lots had been created out of the community's central 600 acre plot, as well as a 'cow-common,' where the settlers' livestock could graze communally. The number of acres given over to pasturage depended on the number of livestock each settler owned. To prevent anyone from claiming more than their fair share of the land, the settlers agreed that in terms of grazing area, five sheep equaled one cow which seems like a sound conclusion.

The colonists were not the only ones living in the neighborhood of Lake Pearl. In 1668, an Indian woman living close to Wollomonopoag turned up in Dedham with her brother and her son to plead with the selectmen for a new property. The Indian woman owned a 10 acre farm squeezed between the private plots of the Wollomonopoag settlers and had begun to feel uncomfortable with her new neighbors. The Dedham government indulged the woman, known to them as Sarah, and gave her a different 10 acre plot on the shore of Uncas Pond.

At the same time that Sarah moved her farm to Uncas Pond, King Philip was arranging to sell more land in Wollomonopoag to the Europeans. The Dedham government was happy to pay his price, realizing that each acre purchased belonged to the community in perpetuity. As the town bought up seven different plots of land, they did not stop to wonder why the Wampanoags were so eager to sell.

During the first five years of 1670s, Wollomponopoag hired a minister and a blacksmith, constructed a small grist mill to grind farmers' grain, and took further steps toward independence from

Dedham. Even though only sixteen families lived in Wollomonopoag, the settlers petitioned the Massachusetts General Court to be incorporated as a town. The settlers argued that the only way to attend town meetings in Dedham center was to travel as much as 20 miles on an extremely rough, wooded track, with no settlements or safe havens along the way. After weighing these concerns, the General Court incorporated the Town of Wrentham on October 17, 1673.

However, almost before the new town of Wrentham had come into its own, it was nearly wiped from the face of the earth by a cataclysmic event masterminded by the former owners of the town's land--King Philip and the Wampanoags. In 1675, three Wampanoags were arrested and hanged in Plymouth for the murder of a Native American who had converted to Christianity. It was a poor move by Plymouth, regarded as an affront to the Wampanoag tribe.

Fighting was quick to break out, and although no single group had declared war, violence quickly escalated—King Philip's War had begun.

King Philip's War came like a bolt from the blue. Town after town went up in smoke, and the 80,000 strong European population of New England soon feared that they would be wiped out entirely, even though they outnumbered the Indians nearly eight to one. Maybe, they speculated, God had seen fit to punish them for sins that they had committed.

The war was unlike anything that the Europeans were accustomed to. Earlier in the 1600s, when the Europeans were fewer in number, they had relied on Indian allies to deal with unruly tribes like the Pequots. Now, though, the Europeans had only each other to rely on. The Europeans were armed with gunpowder and firearms, but the Indians were no longer as impotent, armed only with stone weapons. Instead, tribes like the Wampanoags had adopted muskets, or converted cast-off iron cooking pots into arrowheads and axes. It was going to be a close fight.

King Philip's warriors were remarkably successful, sweeping down to snuff out settlement after settlement, especially along the frontier, destroying towns like Springfield, Hadley, and Lancaster. But even long-settled communities near the coast were not immune. For instance, King Philip even went so far as to attack the second most important 'city' in New England, laying siege to Plymouth. King Philip's initial success stemmed from his alliances with other tribes. He had managed to convince the powerful Narragansetts to put aside previous quarrels and join in the war.

Settlers in Wrentham could see the writing on the wall. The town and its inhabitants might not survive an attack. Rather than wait around for enemy warriors to arrive, the settlers loaded their animals with provisions and hastened women and children to the comparative safety of Dedham. It was probably a timely move. A war party of Narragansetts torched Medfield, and laid siege to a stone fort that served as a last refuge for Medfield residents.

However, the Narragansetts took a pause from their destruction that was to prove fatal. Scouring the Wrentham woods for a lost horse, a man named Rocket spotted a group of 42 Narragansett warriors. He trailed them at a discreet distance until nightfall. Stopping to rest, the war party camped on a rocky outcropping in northern Wrentham far from the center of town, a place in present day Franklin now known as Indian Rock.

Rocket raced back to Wrentham and recruited a dozen men under the command of Captain Robert Ware, whom he led back to the Indian camp. By dawn, the camp was surrounded. As the Indians awoke, a signal was given for the small group to open fire. The crack of muskets startled the Indians, producing an immediate panic. Acting rather than thinking, and with their escape route cut off, most of the Indians left unscathed by the first volley tried to escape off the steep side of the rock, falling to their deaths, or breaking bones in the fall. The seriously wounded warriors were finished off by subsequent volleys from the volunteers atop the rock. One or two Indians escaped death, and fled the scene, spreading word of the English victory. Subsequently, a war party returned and torched the abandoned town of Wrentham in revenge, leaving only two houses standing.

The war cost the Indians more than the English. Six hundred settlers were dead across the region, but the Indians had lost three thousand of their number. Many more were executed or sold into slavery. King Philip himself was killed, rather ironically, by a fellow Native American, albeit one who had converted to Christianity and sided with the English. His body was beheaded, drawn and quartered, and his head put up as a grisly display in Plymouth for twenty years. Although Wrentham had burnt to the ground, one of the triumphant volunteers had reason to be happy. Rocket was awarded an annual pension by the General Court, for his vigilance and swift action in thwarting the Indians.

Back in Dedham once again, the Wrentham settlers were left wondering about the future of their town. With virtually every building torched, and crops neglected or destroyed, did it even make sense to return? Although years of hard work were undone, the townspeople were also better situated than they had been before. In the aftermath of the war, the local Indian threat was at an end—a fact not lost on town fathers. The Indian defeat opened up thousands of acres of new land for the English to sell.

The settlers ultimately voted to return and rebuild Wrentham from the ground up. Ten years after the war, in 1685, the town premiered a new meetinghouse and set aside 25 acres for a school. Most of the farmhouses destroyed in the war had been rebuilt and crops replanted. The exact history of some buildings is unclear because of a lack of written records, but the Hawes family is believed to have built their farmhouse in the aftermath of the war with future Indian attacks in mind. The family's garrison house survived well into the 20th century, and was considered the oldest house in town for decades.

As the men of the town rebuilt the settlement, their families remained in Dedham. When the families relocated back to Wrentham in 1684, young men grown used to the relative excitement of Dedham began to pose a problem. These "large and saucy," boys (as Mortimer Blake described them in his 19th century history) chose to skip religious meetings in favor of adventure. The insubordination continued into the 1690s, when the town appointed two watchmen to guard the town road at night, and to herd young people to services each Sunday.

At the time, new townspeople were arriving from Medfield, and settling in the northwest part of town. The Medfielders were soon putting up houses and cutting down trees to feed the water-powered saw mill being built on Mine Brook.

Ever since European settlement began in the 1620s and 1630s, New Englanders had faced an extreme shortage of hard currency. Most trading involved swaps between towns and tribes, for example, furs in exchange for guns, corn in exchange for nails, or even school lessons. Some things, though, were simply too difficult to produce easily in New England. For example, bed frames were sometimes imported from England—a tremendous expense for poor farmers.

Although bed frames were expensive, other aspects of farming life were getting easier. After decades of wolf hunting, shrinking wolf populations were allowing farmers to put horses and cattle out to pasture with less supervision. Especially along Mine Brook, wide, wet meadows made ideal grazing land for herds. These early 'ranchers,' were able to herd their livestock to the coast each year, loading animals onto ships bound for British sugar plantations in the Caribbean, where soldiers, planters, and slaves hungrily awaited fresh beef.

Cattle were simply too valuable for most farmers to eat on a regular basis. Instead, families got by on every concoction of corn imaginable. Corn bannock and corn mash were supplemented with pease porridge, rye bread, bacon fat, and from time to time wild game, washed down with the tremendous amounts of beer.

By the 1700s the new village on Mine Brook, was generating much of the Wrentham's business. Two sawmills churned out boards, cattle waded around in the swamps, and on higher ground corn stalks took root. Residents were still subject to Wrentham's laws, but felt increasingly independent from the rest of the town.

A few miles to the west, similar ideas were going through the heads of a few hundred Dedham residents. Dedham was still one of the largest towns in the area, but was no longer as geographically cohesive. Fragments of the town left behind as new towns were set up, continued to pay taxes to the selectmen in far off Dedham center.

In 1719, the farmers in one isolated part of Dedham opted to become the Town of Bellingham. From the start, the town had a strong ally in Boston—Edward Rawson, Secretary of the Commonwealth. Rawson owned a third of the town, in the form of a 6,000 acre farm.

Bellingham's move was not lost on residents of western Wrentham. Settled far from the Wrentham church, they were still forced to pay individual contributions to the parish. Since the distance to the town center made participation in the parish difficult or impossible, nineteen families joined in demanding that the Wrentham government repay their contribution.

The Wrentham selectmen were not quick to give the group a reply, and as the families waited, some of their number became impatient. John Pond and 12 others drafted a petition, demanding that western Wrentham be merged with Medway—a community that was actually closer to them. The petition failed, so instead Pond pushed for western Wrentham to be made a precinct—a semi-autonomous community within the larger town of Wrentham.

Both the petition for precinct status, and a second attempt to join Medway faltered, and the 1720s passed with local families still hoping for a change. The Wrentham selectmen patched together a compromise that lasted for a few years, in which school and church services would rotate between the town center and western Wrentham. While the agreement did not cover all of Pond's demands, it at least democratized the trouble of attending church services--now everyone in town was far from church during at least part of the year. Some people living in western Wrentham were pleased, but Pond and company remained unsatisfied and renewed their petition to join Medway. In fact, the new arrangement seemingly increased the fervency of the northwestern residents' attempts to break away. Pond's original band of 12, hard-core, pro-separation residents grew to 46 by the 1730s. With more and more names scrawled on the petitions being dispatched to Wrentham center and Boston, the General Court finally took notice of Pond and his supporters, and sent a committee to investigate the matter. The committee recommended generally in favor of autonomy for the northwestern residents, but it was not until December 23, 1737 that real progress was made. The efforts of John Pond and his son had paid off, and the governor signed into existence Wrentham's second precinct.

The new second precinct (the future town of Franklin) was large, a rectangle four and a half miles wide, and six and a half miles from north to south. On a daily basis, little changed, but residents gained a greater voice in community matters. One of the first orders of business was building a set of bridges over the Charles River to Medway. At the time, in the 1730s, the Charles River still flowed directly to the ocean, and during the spring was alive with potbellied migratory fish called alewives, swimming 80 miles upriver to spawn in the second precinct's Populatic Pond.

No doubt these fish must have been a welcome supplement to the local diet and underscored the continued attractiveness of the second precinct to its settlers.

Chapter 3:

Making a Municipality

...Rather than confronting issues as significant as slavery, locals kept themselves busy with hymnal arguments...

In January, 1738, the residents of the brand new precinct decided to hire a preacher and planned to build a meeting house—what would become Franklin's first community center. The meeting house had a double purpose, serving as a center for government and for Puritan church meetings. But setting up a church was not easy, especially in the 1730s. The congregation needed to receive letters of approval from the Wrentham church, and pray throughout the winter for divine guidance.

Three ministers from Medfield, Wrentham, and Medway certified the church's existence, and left the business of choosing a minister to the residents. Sixty people voted to hire Reverend Haven, granting him 60 acres of prime farmland in exchange for his services. Haven was named minister in November, by visiting church elders from as far away as Boston; he kept his post for 16 years, until he died of tuberculosis in 1754.

Even as the church and the community's first minister were being approved, a succession of surveyors was brought in to find the precinct's exact center. After all, one of the main reasons for the precinct's creation was the distance of western Wrentham residents from the town center. No one wanted to repeat the mistake by creating inequality in the precinct. The spot picked to be the center was set aside as public land for grazing—creating a common—and used as a site for the meeting house. However, a few years after the first survey, a second surveyor claimed that the true center of the town was actually in the middle of Darius Morse's 'mud-pond,' close by the common.

Most early records of the precinct have to do with the community church. There was little new happening in the area besides church business. Church records were well kept because of their official nature and Massachusetts still maintained Congregationalism (the more modern name for Puritanism) as its official religion.

As services were held in the new meetinghouse, the prominent Pond family began to stir up trouble. The issue at hand seems extremely minor looking back from the 21st century, but it was enough to divide the community for half a generation. The Congregationalists had sung the same hymns since the 1640s, not always according to the words published in the hymnal, and were in no hurry to change their tune.

Reverend Haven pushed for his congregation to sing hymns as they were written in the hymn book, an idea so outlandish that David Pond was willing to defy him. Pond was thrown out of church, and refused to rejoin for 13 years, fuming about hymns the whole time.

The Ponds could afford to be obstinate. Oliver Pond, one of David's relatives was possibly the "wealthiest" man in the precinct. He owned several farms and controlled the grist mill. In addition, Pond owned a tavern in the community center (where Vallee's Jewelry is today), and made enough money off of travelers to build a house for his wife and 13 children that stands to this day on Rt. 140. The new house allowed Pond to stay close to his mill in what is now Unionville, the village along Mine Brook that he had helped to create. In addition to grist and saw mills, a different group of entrepreneurs built an iron forge to smelt bog iron from the swamps around the brook (lending Forge Hill its name).

One of the weirdest stories involving Unionville and the Pond family is the story of the 'witch,' Moll Sheckel. According to 20th century Franklin historian and history teacher, James Johnston (present day owner of the Oliver Pond house), Sheckel was a reputed witch living close to the Pond grist mill. At one point, Sheckel supposedly offered to protect Pond's mill by casting protective enchantments. In exchange for her services, she would be allowed to grind enough grain to support herself.

After turning Sheckel's offer down, the Ponds became convinced that their house was cursed—their bread oven ruined their loaves, and their cows stopped giving milk. Rumors spread across the second precinct, convincing even the local physician—Dr. Metcalf—and his wife. Metcalf's wife believed that her loaves were turning sour due to a curse, and burnt them in the oven to rid her house of black magic. The story is probably apocryphal, but in a small community such as the second precinct, bizarre rumors about eccentric neighbors were probably quick to spread.

Old superstitions seem almost laughable, but other colonial ideas are even more difficult to understand. In 1754, Governor Shirley ordered a census of the colony's slave population (slavery remained legal in Massachusetts until after the American Revolution). The survey showed that 13 slaves lived in Wrentham—perhaps a few in the second precinct. Wrentham had fewer slaves than Bellingham (21), Medway (58), and Medfield (44). By and large, these enslaved individuals were of African descent, usually serving as domestic servants rather than farm-hands.

Rather than confronting issues as significant as slavery, locals kept themselves busy with hymnal arguments through the 1760s, until the eve of the American Revolution. The British government slowly moved to limit local government, but their most intolerable action was the Boston Port Bill of 1774, that prevented farmers in the countryside from exporting cattle and grain to the Caribbean.

Furious with the British government, idle local farmers laid in a store of gunpowder for the municipal cannon, and sent men to the re-organized General Court in Salem (where towns agreed to put together a force of 12,000 militiamen), and refused to pay royal taxes. Rebelliousness extended to helping deserters from the British ships in Boston harbor. For example, a conscript named John Newton swam three miles to shore from a British ship, moored in Boston harbor. His midnight escape almost cost him his life. When he reached shore, exhausted, he was spirited into the countryside and hidden at a safe-house in Franklin. Newton ultimately settled in Franklin, and became a fixture of local life.

When war broke out in April, 1775, five companies of Wrentham militiamen marched north to join the fighting. Many of these men went on to become members of the Continental Army, including 17 from the Pond family alone.*

The exact number of local people in military service is debatable, because of poor record keeping. Some were listed in militia records, while their service to the Continental Army was ignored.

For people who sympathized with the British government, life quickly became uncomfortable. Aldis, a Franklin storekeeper, was suspected of being a British sympathizer because of his friendship with an officer in the British army. When he died in 1775, a mob ransacked his store, stealing all of his property including his personal papers, although none of his documents proved any link to British interests.

Asa Aldis, five years old at the time of his father's death went to live with a branch of the Pond family in Medway. After the war ended, Captain Goldsbury—a prominent Franklin man with known British sympathies who had fled to Nova Scotia—returned the storekeeper's papers to Asa. Goldsbury had smuggled them out of the country for safekeeping during the war years. Because no evidence of anti-American activity could be found, almost all of the storekeeper's remaining property was returned to his son. With the money, Aldis went on to graduate from Brown University and become one of Vermont's first Chief Justices!

The preparation of volunteer militias for the conflict gave people their first taste of combat since King Philip's War, and led communities

* At least one member of the Pond family, Penuel Pond died in captivity on a British prison hulk in New York. Another nearly starved to death in a converted sugar warehouse used to hold prisoners.

to push for greater independence. The second precinct petitioned Wrentham to become a separate town, in 1777.

Approval was given in 1778, and a new group of selectmen went to work coming up with a name for their new town. The first name they chose was Exeter. In fact, in founding documents, the town name was written in as Exeter, Massachusetts. But at the last moment, the selectmen had a change of heart, scratching out Exeter and replacing it with Franklin, in honor of the famed American statesman, Benjamin Franklin. It was a good name for a town in open rebellion against Britain, and perhaps sounded more American than Exeter.

Franklin—a new town with a new government -- had plenty of work to get done, including approval of a new Massachusetts constitution, and getting itself established on a sound fiscal footing in the midst of the financial uncertainties of the times.

Even with peace, and both local and national independence, there were still some reminders of the war that had just ended. French troops that had helped the Americans to win the war headed home in 1782, coming very close to Franklin. On December 31, thousands of French soldiers under the command of General Rochambeau camped at Lake Archer in Wrentham. The encampment stretched for almost a mile, from the lake's shore to the center of town. It was an incredible moment for locals, watching the world's most powerful army making camp alongside their well-worked cornfields.

No matter how much pride and camaraderie residents might have felt as they drank and ate with the French troops, there was no escaping the truth—Franklin was only a tiny hamlet, loyal to a loosely formed confederation of newly independent colonies, working toward an uncertain and fragile future as the world's only democracy.

Chapter 4:

Sense Instead of Sound

...Dr. Emmons harshly criticized James Mann at his funeral. In essence, he told the Mann family that their son had deserved to drown...

Four years after the American Revolution ended, news from the United States began to travel across the Atlantic Ocean once again. Still residing n Paris, Benjamin Franklin heard, for the first time, that a town had been named in his honor. In local lore, it was at this point that the new town asked its namesake for funds to purchase a meetinghouse bell. Never one to disappoint, Franklin did give the town a gift, but not the one that the selectmen had hoped for. In place of a bell, Franklin sent his famous gift of books, believing that future generations would be, "More fond of sense than sound."

One of Franklin's colleagues in England, Dr. Price, selected the books and sent them by ship to Massachusetts. The original gift of 116 books went over well with the town, and the community decided to buy an additional 100 volumes – a tremendous investment for a frontier town. The collection featured a range of influential works, including famous 18th century philosophers such as Locke and Montesquieu.

In fact, neighboring Wrentham had one of the earliest parish lending libraries in the colonies, and had served as temporary home for Brown University's books during the Revolution. At first, Franklin modeled its collection after Wrentham's, open only to members of the local parish (which included everyone in town). However, in 1788, the selectmen decided to make the library available to everyone, marking the first true public library in the United States. The first librarian was Dr. Emmons, a famous Congregationalist minister appointed to the local parish in 1773.

The town built a new meetinghouse in the 1780s, and especially in Unionville began to see a growth in business. Although its grazing land and bog iron helped to bring in some money, Unionville appears to have been one of the poorest areas in town due to its poor cropland. In 1782, Timothy Rockwood began to change that image, opening the town's first drug store and a grocery store to serve the village. In 1800, Nathaniel Thayer and his family moved to Unionville, and started out in manufacturing alongside the Makepeaces and Rockwoods. Two Thayer men, Davis and Asa moved to Franklin Center and set up a straw products business. With money from that venture, Asa started the Franklin Hotel, by the common, one of the first inns in town.

During the 1780s, Daniel Shays and a band of poverty stricken farmers staged a small revolt in western Massachusetts. The revolt was unsuccessful, but it was enough to scare the weak national government into writing a stronger constitution. Even when a new federal government was set up in the 1790s, many people were uneasy about the extreme violence taking place in France, as revolutionaries overthrew the king and demanded democracy. However, one Franklin man, inspired by the ideals of the French Revolution, decided to act.

David McLane was born in Attleboro, and spent much of his adult life as a merchant in North Carolina. The same year as Shays' Rebellion, he married in Franklin. His wife gave birth to a daughter, Rebecca. Sadly, though, McLane's wife passed away and he was hit with financial troubles in the early 1790s. At the time, French ambassador Adet was traveling the country with a group of emissaries, trying desperately to whip up support for the French Revolution. McLane bought into Adet's message and came to believe that the greatest work to be done in North America was the overthrow of the British government in Quebec, and the liberation of the colony's French speaking citizens.

Remarkably, McLane was convinced and decided to take unilateral action. He packed his bags and traveled to Quebec City to try to enlist a group of volunteers. Together, they would storm the city garrison and topple the British authorities. In Quebec City, McLane managed to recruit a few people for his cause, but did not fill them in on all of the details. Nor was he, it seems, particularly cautious. One of those involved in the conspiracy was John Black, a shipbuilder and coincidentally a member of the Provincial Parliament. When Black learned the full extent of McLane's plans, he promptly turned the American over to the British authorities.

McLane was sentenced to death for sedition, and the sentence was carried out in public in a very grisly fashion. McLane was hanged outside the city walls, his limbs and head were severed, and his internal organs burnt. Black was rewarded with land, but gained a reputation as a British informant, ultimately dying in poverty. McLane's execution has the distinction of being the last known example of hanging, drawing and quartering in North America.

As an adult, Rebecca McLane recovered her father's remains through persistence, and had them buried in Franklin, with Dr. Emmons presiding over the funeral. The last North American victim of this medieval punishment is still buried in an unmarked grave in town.

The same year that McLane traveled to Canada, the Mann family welcomed a child who would change the course of American history. Horace Mann was born on the family farm at the Four Corners, on May 4, 1796. The Mann homestead was located where the Horace Mann

Plaza is today. In the 1790s, it was known as the Mann Plain because of the land's general flatness. The family owned a two-story colonial house, heated in winter by a central chimney, and surrounded by outbuildings for livestock.

Horace's parents were strict and reserved, even harsh, but they instilled their son with strong morals from a young age. The Four Corners was an intersection of two major roads, known today as Rt. 140 and King Street. The Mann family's strategic location helped to broaden Horace's world view—on one occasion, a young woman visited the family, displaying tremendous skill in Latin recitation that inspired his lifelong interest in the language.

Horace was an eager learner, but until the age of 15, he had only a few weeks of formal schooling, though he was far from being an illiterate bumpkin. Much of what he learned as a young man came from Benjamin Franklin's donated books. Although he devoured almost all the books in the library, he looked back on the experience with regret. "I wasted my youthful ardor upon its martial pages, and learned to glory in war, which both reason and conscience have since taught me to consider almost universally a crime. Oh! When will men learn to redeem that childhood in their offspring which was lost to themselves?" Mann was a pacifist ahead of his time.

By nature, Horace Mann seems to have been a gentle person, but his hatred for Dr. Emmons was legendary. His 12 year old brother, James Mann, drowned in Uncas Pond, while swimming alone. The death of James Mann*-- and the events of his funeral -- would haunt Horace for the rest of his life.

Dr. Emmons harshly criticized James Mann at his funeral. In essence, he told the Mann family that their son had *deserved* to drown for skipping church on the Sabbath. The event left lasting scars. According to one of Horace Mann's lifelong friends (as related in his 1904 biography), "He [Horace Mann] said he [James Mann] was a charming boy, and that his death immediately brought home to his heart the terribleness of the theological views in which he was educated... A strange fascination would impel him, Sunday after Saturday, to find in Watt's hymn book, and read over and over again, a certain verse, which must be eliminated in modern editions, for I cannot find it; but it depicted the desolation of a solitary soul in eternity, rudderless and homeless."

There seems to be some conflict as to the name of Horace Mann's brother. In Mann's biography, his brother's name is recorded as James, while James C. Johnston, Jr. an author of books on Franklin history, believed his name to be Stephen.

"He thought he could see in his mother's face a despair beyond the grief of losing the mortal life of her son; and when, at the funeral, Dr. Emmons, instead of suggesting a thought of consoling character, improved the opportunity to address a crowd of young persons present on the topic of 'dying unconverted,' and he heard his mother groan, a crisis took place in his experience..."

Dr. Emmons, the figure at the center of it all, was a controversial preacher. "More than toil, or by privation of any natural taste, was the inward joy of my youth blighted by theological inculcations. The pastor of the church in Franklin was the somewhat celebrated Dr. Emmons, who not only preached to his people, but ruled them for more than fifty years. He was an extreme Calvinist-- a brilliant but often extremely unkind person. He expounded the doctrines of total depravity, election and reprobation, and not only the eternity, but the extremity, of hell torments, unflinchingly and in their most terrible significance; while he rarely if ever descanted upon the joys of heaven, and never, to my recollection, upon the essential and necessary happiness of a virtuous life," wrote Horace Mann later in his life.

Dr. Emmons was a well-known preacher, and even in death had as many admirers as detractors. Duane Hamilton Hurd (who authored an 1884 history of Norfolk County), wrote that, "In one aspect Dr. Emmons has been and still is misrepresented. He was not curt, dogmatic, and repellent. He was not unsocial and austere to his people, nor a bugbear to the young. He was affable, genial, and witty, and enjoyed a good joke as keenly as anyone." However, for many people, such as Horace Mann, the only alternative to Dr. Emmons and his strict Congregationalist faith was conversion to Unitarianism or Universalism—two, new, similar faiths.

Reverend Jacob Ide (Dr. Emmons grandson, who spoke at the town centennial in 1878) said of his famous grandfather, "...I suppose that I am placed here as a relic of Dr. Emmons' ministry, and am expected to represent it by contrast. I hoped that Edison would have perfected his phonograph so that it could be placed on Dr. Emmons' tombstone and he could have spoken for himself. I confess, sir, that I am proud of my grandfather; but I am afraid, if he were here to-day, that he would not be willing to reciprocate the compliment...Dr. Emmons' ministry must certainly be regarded as a *successful* ministry, for he made his people do as he pleased...Men carried home from the sanctuary [church] something that was not only worth remembering, but something that was not easy to forget."

Emmons was not an easy man to forget, it seems, and with good reason. He spent 54 years as Franklin's minister, running the public library out of his barn, as a sideline. By the time he died in 1827, Horace Mann had already left town.

After leaving Franklin, Horace Mann studied at Brown University and was admitted to the bar as an attorney. But the world had more in store for Mann than life as a village lawyer. After joining the Unitarian faith, Horace Mann gathered up local supporters and ran for office, representing Dedham in the General Court. Mann rose quickly through the ranks of state government, becoming president of the Massachusetts Senate.

Along with Dorothea Dix and other reformers, Mann created the state's first insane asylum in Worcester, ending the cruel treatment and jailing of people with mental illness.

In the 1830s, Mann was named the head of Massachusetts Board of Education. As a child, he himself had been unable to attend school, and he had paid his way through Brown University by braiding straw hats. He believed that free, standardized, public education was essential.

Studying the public education system of the German kingdom, Prussia, Mann created a plan for Massachusetts*. In his new plan, 'normal' schools would train teachers in modern methods of teaching that involved fewer beatings and more lessons for students. Students were also required to attend school up until a certain age. The first normal schools (present day state universities) were soon opened in Bridgewater and Framingham. To normalize schooling, Mann planned to implement standardized testing and standard curriculums.

Massachusetts representative (and former president) John Quincy Adams died in 1848, and Mann was voted in to replace him. In Washington, Mann represented the anti-slavery initiatives of the Whig Party. The capital buzzed with debate about slavery, leaving Mann exhausted. In 1852 he returned to Massachusetts to run as an anti-slavery candidate for governor. Losing the race, he was appointed president of Antioch College in Ohio. Mann passed away in 1859, and was buried in Providence, but his educational system lived on and spread across the country.

Meanwhile, other developments began to unsettle the old ways in Franklin.

In the 1790s, a woman named Hannah Metcalf who worked for a Providence millinery shop producing hats, discovered a valuable secret. The shop imported braided straw hats from Europe, a very popular item with women during the summertime. One day, Metcalf unraveled a straw hat and uncovered the secret of braiding the straw. In 1799, a

*From early colonial times, many New England towns had informal public schools, supported by the local government, but these schools varied greatly in what they taught, and access to education was still limited.

group of girls from Providence arrived at a private school in Wrentham, and taught the other students their braiding method—the same method that Metcalf had spread throughout Providence. Word spread, and straw braiding spread across southeastern Massachusetts. By 1812, this became the basis for small trading stores that opened up in town to swap goods for bonnets, made by local women. It was a harbinger of things to come.

Chapter 5:

Muster Days

...Trumpets blared, drums rattled, horses reared and snorted, children screamed, ramrods, forgotten in the hurried loading, hurtled through the poplars...

Life could get pretty tedious in 19th century Franklin. Working days were long and most work was not very stimulating, but at least locals could count on a few diversions to deal with their boredom. Church life kept people occupied on the weekends, but even the most pious farmer in the 1820s could apparently stomach only so much prayer and Biblical reading.

The Fourth of July was celebrated fervently by everyone in town. In 1823, a special Independence Day picnic was held at Indian Rock; local notables gave speeches while everyone enjoyed the view. After all, with most of Massachusetts cleared of trees, Indian Rock afforded a great vantage point from which Blue Hill and Mt. Wachusett were visible.

Even the Fourth of July was outdone by militia drills. Franklin had two militia companies, one for the north of town and one for the south. Militia drills were probably the most exciting events in Franklin in the early 1800s, at least if Mortimer Blake is to be believed. "The May trainings were the times for public comparison—when both companies manoeuvred [sic] at the opposite ends of the Common, and marched around Davis Thayer's store and Dr. Emmon's house, and the voices of the captains could be heard throughout the whole distance...Training day was usually enlivened by a troop of cavalry, enrolled within the town, which pranced and curveted among the sweet fern at the south end of the Common."

Usually, the common was used to graze livestock, but on a few days each year the cattle and sheep were herded away and replaced by militiamen.

"...The Franklin Artillery struck the deepest awe into boyish hearts. It included many members from Wrentham, but its gun-house, cannons, tumbril and horse furniture were on Franklin Common, and here it paraded according to the law." The Franklin Artillery's uniforms were showy, consisting of, "Dark blue and slightly trimmed uniform," with, "Red tipped plumes," and, "Flashing swords." The Franklin Artillery was armed with, "lumbering brass four-pounders [cannons]." Mortimer Blake also described the elite of Franklin's militia. "...The height of excitement was reached when the Franklin Cadets appeared.

They had been drilling for weeks behind the powder- house hill under a Captain Partridge, from some military school, and believed themselves to be the elite of the militia."

The Franklin Cadets acted the part, dressed in expensive uniforms that rivaled those of the Franklin Artillery. In fact, the Franklin Cadets were not just putting on a show. "The Franklin Cadets, the Wrentham Guards, and the Bellingham Rifles were the flower of the...Norfolk County Regiment." When autumn arrived and the crops were harvested, Franklinites turned out to witness the muster of the militia, an impressive annual event. On the day before the muster, men from the militia would cordon off the Common with ropes. Others worked into the night setting up tents and refreshment stands.

The following morning, the town militia, and hundreds of spectators flocked to the Common by foot and wagon. "Tents and marquees were hastily pitched around the meeting-house and on the west side of the Common. Luncheon boxes and extra garments were stowed in them, guards set, and at six o'clock the long roll from a score or less of kettle-drums called the companies together to the turmoil of the day. Drill, evolutions and marching displayed the skill of the captains, and astonished the fast- gathering crowds until 9 o'clock, when, at the vociferous shouting of the adjutant, the musical squads headed their companies up to the toe-line already described. The musicians then gathered at the head of the regiment near the gun- house to receive the colonel and his staff whenever they should emerge from the tavern near at hand."

"On their appearance and reception the wings wheeled into an enclosing square, with the officers in the center, and the chaplain, on horseback, prayed for the country and the protection of life and limb." After more maneuvering and an inspection by the town's officers, the militiamen and spectators broke for lunch. "At one o'clock came dinner in tent, booth, on the grass, anywhere, hilariously moistened—possibly with venerable cider..." In other words, after a morning of marching and gawking, Franklinites ate lunch for two hours and perhaps drank a bit too much hard apple cider.*

"...At three o'clock a big gun and a solemn cavalcade of colonel and staff with chaplain and surgeon called the scattered bands into line for the grand finale—the sham fight. This used to be a great exploit of strategic skill. Sometimes the infantry attempted to capture the guns and artillery; sometimes, divided into two equal battalions, they furiously bombarded each other; sometimes a tribe of pretentious

*According to Thomas Maki, author of Men of Franklin, local temperance advocates William Makepeace Thayer and Dr. Amory Hunting managed to limit the sale of alcohol during haying and harvesting season.

Indians rushed from behind Dr. Pratt's barn with original and indescribable yells upon the cavalry only to be ignominiously chased back to their invisible wigwams...Trumpets blared, drums rattled, horses reared and snorted, children screamed, ramrods, forgotten in the hurried loading, hurtled through the poplars, till a cloud of villainous saltpetre enwrapped in suffocating folds soldiers, spectators, booths and landscape, and until cartridge boxes were emptied and military furore was satiated."

"The hubbub subsided about five o'clock into an occasional pop from tardy muskets...and the crowd took up their winding way—to some very winding—to their supper less homes. And so ended the autumnal muster, but we boys thought it a great day."

The 1820s were an excellent time to belong to the Franklin militia. America was not embroiled in any wars and Indian attacks in Massachusetts had ended nearly a century earlier. The militia encouraged local pride. Families enjoyed watching the autumnal muster and the militia drills in the spring. The prominent men in town were usually captains or colonels in the militia and those involved could be proud of defending their community, even if there was actually little threat to its existence. The fact that a town like Franklin--with only 1,630 citizens in 1820--owned cannons, and organized its own cavalry and militia, dressed in the finest uniforms that money could buy, seems remarkable from the vantage point of the 21st century.

Years of drilling almost paid off in 1840, when violence broke out in Rhode Island. To the south, the state government in Providence clung to an antique colonial charter that prevented citizens who did not own property, from voting. Over 100,000 were ineligible to vote, and only a few very wealthy voters controlled the government. Suffrage groups held mass meetings, demanding a change. Thomas Wilson Dorr, was the son of a wealthy Woonsocket mill owner, and an opponent of the state law.

When legislators in Providence refused to listen, Dorr formed the People's Party, and held a convention to draw up a new constitution, and form a new government. Under the new constitution, men who did not own property were given the right to vote, and quickly elected Dorr as governor. Unfortunately, Rhode Island faced a sticky situation—two governors and two governments claimed to lead one very small state.

Both governors tried to rally Washington to their side, but violence soon broke out. Governor King declared martial law, and attempted to stop Dorr and his party, leading to a six week civil war. Franklin had no local newspaper at the time, so local opinion is difficult to judge; however, the unrest was big news around the country, and a cause of concern for President Tyler. He decided not to intervene with federal troops, but ordered Massachusetts and Connecticut to stand ready to invade Rhode Island. Although state militias never intervened, and the conflict came to a quick end, Franklin's own men would have been amongst the first to cross into Woonsocket, to strike at the heart of Dorr's rebellion.

News of Dorr's rebellion would have spread quickly up the Smithfield road (currently Washington St.) one of the two main thoroughfares, and the only main road leading to Rhode Island from Franklin.

Roads were important for more than just news and, as the century passed, many were gradually improved. Current day Rt. 140 was the Taunton and Worcester Rd. Both roads were toll-free, but probably poorly maintained compared with privately owned toll roads, such as the Hartford and Dedam Turpike in Medway. Toll roads stayed in operation up until the railroad expansion of the 1840s, although even in New England, particularly at night, such highways were often unsafe to travel because of robbers.

In New England, highway robbery was not uncommon. Tom Cook, a Robin Hood character raided wagons all around New England giving away grain meal to poor farmers. But most highway robbers were not so gentlemanly. Cyrus Knowlton, the keeper of a toll booth in Roxbury found himself disturbed at midnight by a gang of robbers who attempted to break into his shack. "I told them I would not [let them in]—Thereupon they stove in the window...I struck [back] with a sword." After menacing him with a pistol, the robbery faltered and the robbers made their escape. Knowlton pursued them, following the trail of blood on the winter snow, but without success. Robberies such as this were not uncommon and made traveling long distances difficult and dangerous. Franklinites would give second thoughts to traveling far beyond town, knowing the danger and the difficulty.

For travelers to Franklin, Thayer's tavern on the Taunton and Worcester highway was always a reliable place to stay the night. Thurston, the proprietor, would have walked each day up the dirt road from his house to his establishment. He might have stopped across the road at the pasture where the stage coach horses were tied up, to make sure that they were well watered, and that they had not broken loose from their hitching posts. Then it would be on to the business of the day. Thurston probably fed wayfarers baked beans, salt pork, steak, stew, bread or biscuits, or some form of corn meal, all washed down with ample quantities of alcohol.

One of the earliest comprehensive maps of the town was produced in 1831, by special order of the selectmen. In 53 years since incorporation, population had only increased by a few hundred people, but industry had blossomed. Remaining stands of trees were being cut down at an alarming rate to feed six saw mills, and to heat 219 houses and 10 "publick" schools. There were three cotton mills, and a thread-needle mill near Populatic Pond, started with profits from Dr. Miller's hospital. The hospital, also located by the pond, attracted patients from across Massachusetts, in search of cures for their many ailments.

One of the town's landmark public schools, the Red Brick Schoolhouse was built in 1833, three years after the map was commissioned. The site where the school was built already had a long history to it. During the 18th century, Dr. Emmons, with a remarkable degree of optimism, had taken a *nine hundred year* lease on the land, and built a wooden school house. Mortimer Blake—future minister and town historian—took charge of the Red Brick School in 1835.

The present brick, one room school house claims to be the oldest continuously operating one room school house in America, although the original claim to be the oldest one room school house in the country proved unsupportable. A school, in Croydon, New Hampshire now seems to have a stronger claim to being the oldest one room school house in the country.

Other improvements came for the town's poorest residents. The selectmen bought a farm by Uncas Pond and set it up as a community poor farm. The Congregationalists improved their facility as well, holding the last service in the meeting house constructed in the 1780s, in 1840. The building was torn down, and parts of it sent across the country. The bell ended up in Paxton, and the pulpit landed in Chicago!

Franklin's large Congregationalist community (those that had stayed in line with Dr. Emmons into the 1820s) decided to build a monument to commemorate the late preacher. An association with members from Dedham and Providence (including the president of Brown University) raised money and placed a monument on the common. At the time, the Congregationalists had free reign to put up monuments on the common, which was still a church property on which parishioners could graze their livestock. However, when the land was given over to the town, the monument was removed to the Union St. Cemetery, where it still stands today.

The Congregationalists could apparently afford to build monuments, but they were missing out on local recruiting. New religious groups were pushing into the Franklin area, diversifying the town's outlook. Cumberland and Sheldonville were home to large Baptist communities, most of whom worked for the Sheldon family as boat-builders (as it turns out, Sheldonville was once a boatbuilding center, in spite of its lack of water). Unitarians and a similar group known as the Universalists were growing in number in Franklin, joined each year by a few more converts from Congregationalism.

The 1840s also introduced the first Catholics to Franklin. The Norfolk Railroad Company built a line through Franklin with the help of hundreds of Irish immigrant 'navvies.' Navvies did long backbreaking work, constructing a rail bed, and building stations along the way. A few families settled by the 1850s, and borrowed the town hall (built in 1842) as a temporary church, until a more permanent location could be found. The town hall was also put to use by Universalists and Methodists, groups that were able to able to afford their own church buildings by the end of the 1850s. The Congregationalist community itself expanded beyond a single church in 1856, with the construction of the South Franklin Meeting House.*

The growing wealth that helped Franklinites to pay for new churches stemmed from entrepreneurs such as the Ray family. The Ray brothers opened their first shoddy mill in Unionville in 1849. Today, we think of shoddy as a general term for something of poor quality. Actually, shoddy is something different. During the 1840s, shoddy was recycled woolen scraps, collected and re-processed into new cloth. Low quality shoddy cloth could be sold locally, or sent south to clothe slaves.

Along with shoddy, the famous straw hat industry also continued to grow, pointing the ways to broader industrial growth in the years to come.

*This building still exists. It is the oldest church in Franklin, and served as the Horace Mann Museum from 1975-2010.

Chapter 6:

The Villagers

...Wadsworth was on the tongues of reporters from as far away as Boston...

As Franklin's population grew, and its industries expanded, people began to cluster within smaller communities focused around mills and railroad stations. The number of villages was never fixed, but Franklin had at least five distinct communities—Franklin Center, Unionville, Caryville, City Mills and Wadsworth.

Franklin Center, as one might guess from the name, was the town center, a dense cluster of shops, a railroad station, several mills, the town hall, and most the of the local churches.

Ranking second to Franklin Center in size and wealth was Unionville, in western Franklin. Some road maps still depict Unionville to this day, and real townies still talk about it. Unionville formed in colonial times, when mills were built along Mine Brook, but the village grew significantly only after the Ray family built their mills. In present day geography, Unionville would include everything along Rt. 140 from Beaver Street to the Forge Park train station and Garelick Farms.

As Franklin's oldest village, other than Franklin Center (dating from before the American Revolution), Unionville grew most rapidly after the Rays moved into the area in the 1840s. Francis, Joseph, and James the sons of Colonel Joseph Ray, who set up the family's first mill in 1839, became partners in the Ray Brothers company, and collaborated to build the Ray shoddy picker. The brothers went in separate directions around 1860, when Francis opened his own mill. Even separately, they remained shareholders.

Caryville, another extinct community, was actually shared between Medway, Bellingham and Franklin. Bellingham had a number of villages, each with a peculiar name to describe its location within the town, or its main product. For example, Rakeville in South Bellingham, produced rakes, and North Bellingham was (as the name implies) located in North Bellingham. Caryville was a cluster of mills built around a dam on both sides of the Charles River. The village took shape in 1813, when Joseph Fairbanks bought water rights, and set up a mill. His grandchildren started a lucrative boot shop with profits from his earlier mill. Caryville had little in common with the rest of Franklin—the village had its own post office, grocery store, and even a school. The folks in Caryville had so little in common with either Bellingham or Franklin, that in 1816, the village actually petitioned the General Court unsuccessfully for incorporation as a town.

City Mills was similar in many ways to Caryville, although its mills clustered close to the Mill River in what is now Norfolk. City Mills, together with Unionville and Caryville generated most of Franklin's money in manufactured goods.

South Franklin, a general description for the agricultural, southern part of town, was home to the tiny farming community of Wadsworth. In spite of its small size, Wadsworth has more recorded about its history than many larger villages such as Caryville, thanks to the diaries of one resident, George Wadsworth. In January, 1857, George Wadsworth, a 20 year old farm hand, bought a 'Pocket Diary for 1857.' The booklet was advertised, "For the use of merchants, manufacturers, mechanics, housekeepers, and professional men." The first eleven pages of the pocket diary included useful information ranging from a list of Sundays in 1857, to lunar phases and eclipses for the year, as well as postage rates.

George's family the Wadsworths, were the founders of the village, and the village centered around their family farms and businesses. Seth Wadsworth, the patriarch of the Wadsworth clan had migrated to Franklin from Milton years earlier. In 1857, he had already exceeded the average life expectancy of most 19th century Americans. He had been born in 1795, and in 1857 he turned 62. Upon arriving in Franklin, Seth Wadsworth had bought farmland in South Franklin on Spring Street, and married Olive Metcalf. Spring Street at the time ran north to south from Unionville, intersecting Washington Street, and running roughly parallel to Prospect Street. With the exception of the Wadsworth property, and a handful of other farms, Spring Street had few houses.

Together, Seth and Olive had four children. The oldest, Mary Wadsworth was born in 1824, while her brother, Joseph H. Wadsworth was born in 1826. After a seven year gap, Olive gave birth to two more children--Nancy Stone Wadsworth in 1833 and George M. Wadsworth in 1836.

During the 1840s and '50s, when the Norfolk Railroad Company built a line to Franklin, the railroad was extended to Wadsworth and out toward Woonsocket. A small railroad station was built in Wadsworth. The station served everyone in South Franklin, and made the Wadsworths a small fortune. The village soon boasted a post office, blacksmith shop, country store, and even a school. By the late 1850s, the Norfolk Railroad Company had been succeeded by the New York and New England Rail Road.

On the south side of the railroad tracks, Spring Street led out to Washington Street. J.B. Whiting lived on the corner, and must have watched each day as children from Wadsworth, and Washington Street walked to the schoolhouse at the corner of Prospect Street. George Wadsworth owned a house south of the railroad tracks. A few yards to the north of his house was the combined store, post office, and railroad station, while in back a barn looked out on an expansive swampy meadow watered by a brook that also fed a shallow pond diagonally south across the street. The blacksmith shop was opposite his house.

On the opposite, northern side of the tracks, George's brother Joseph tended an orchard that abutted the tracks. The orchard, Joseph Wadsworth's barn and his "House on Hill" (further up the street) were both on the eastern side of Spring Street. Opposite the orchard was a railroad platform and a watering tank for steam locomotives. Between Joseph's house and the orchard, a well was used to draw water for the railroad. In fact, there was also a spring behind Joseph's house that may have lent Spring Street its name.

On a foul-weather day, Sunday, January 18, George made his first entry in the diary. "Cold and clear- 11 degrees below zero, no meeting at the school house, went to Mr. Phersons in the morning. Snowed the evening," he wrote. The South Franklin Congregationalist meetinghouse was still incomplete, and in the meantime, George and his neighbors resorted to meeting in the village schoolhouse on the corner of Prospect and Washington Street.

The blizzard conditions continued into the following day, and George spent another idle day with his friend Mr. Pherson, who lived on Washington Street. On Tuesday, as his cousin made him a new shirt, George dug snow out of Mr. Pherson's cellar and did chores. The late January snowstorm disrupted railroad traffic to Wadsworth. Mail deliveries were delayed for nine days, school was cancelled, and not a single locomotive came for a week. When it finally arrived, the locomotive had a broken snowplow. More than 40 passengers were forced to disembark, and eat dinner at the South Franklin station.

Day-to-day existence in Wadsworth centered on church and farm life, neighbors and family. Meetings were frequently held at the South Franklin schoolhouse, the South Franklin Congregational church (built 1856), or the Lyceum in West Wrentham, where young farmers such as George were often joined by lady friends for an evening of spirited debate. By rail and road, George, Joseph, and the other Wadsworths often traveled to Franklin Center, Woonsocket, Holliston, and even as far away as Milton and Millville on business and to see acquaintances.

But visiting could wait when there was work to be done. George worked hard to keep his house and his farm in order, but also shared responsibility with his brother Joseph for running the country store. Adding to these obligations, George always found time to help his circle of friends and neighbors when they were in need. On any given day, especially during the harvest in September and October, he might have been gathering hay, raking cranberries, picking apples, digging potatoes, cutting and loading chestnut and oak wood at the saw mill on Washington Street, or any number of other tasks. George was a farmer who thought nothing of splitting a half-cord of wood in a morning, spending the afternoon bent over picking beans, or butchering hogs with his neighbors.

The regimen of hard work never ended in Wadsworth. December 25th, 1857-- Christmas Day--George spent the day in the Wadsworth store, accompanied his brother to the family wood lot to cut fuel for the stove, and attended writing school in the evening. Winter in Wadsworth was marked with continued visits to the Lyceum, frequent trips to the pond to 'fish' for muskrat beneath the ice, and to the wood lot for firewood. During a thaw in early January 1858, George brought in his beehive, to warm by the stove. In his diary, he recorded, "Took care of bees, we thought they were dead. They got quite lively." One can only imagine what a hive of 'lively' bees must have been like in a warm parlor.

Trains were often delayed during inclement winter weather. Many times, railroad passengers and other travelers stayed over in Wadsworth. For example, George was visited in January 1858 by an unintelligible Dutchman who needed a roof over his head.

Once in a great while, Wadsworth villagers were distracted from their work and social commitments by unforeseen events. The founding of a Parish Committee to run the South Franklin church, in 1855, and the creation of an independent South Franklin Lyceum (essentially a debating society) had drawn little attention outside of the village, but on Tuesday January 18, 1859, Wadsworth was on the tongues of reporters from as far away as Boston.

The story of what happened that night was splashed on the pages of the *Woonsocket Daily Traveller*, the *Woonsocket Patriot*, and the *Boston Traveller*. Susan Whiting was described as, "an active and intelligent young lady," 16 years old in 1859. She lived about three-quarters of a mile from Wadsworth station with her parents, at the time. Only a mile away from Susan Whiting's house lived Otis Wales, Jr. a prosperous South Franklin farmer. One of Wales' sons married Susan's older sister. In the aftermath of the marriage, Susan fell in love with Wales' other son, Jonathon, a mild-mannered, 28 year old farm boy. Even though Susan's parents opposed the match, Susan and Jonathon were secretly engaged. Jonathon gave his lover gifts such as a gold watch and chain.

But the relationship was not as permanent as Jonathon might have hoped. Six or eight weeks after their secret engagement, Susan decided to follow her parents' wishes and ended her engagement to Jonathon, returning all of the jewelry that she had received. To say that he was heartbroken would be to put it mildly. As the *Boston Daily Traveller's* special reporter wrote, "From this time he began to change, acting listless and growing haggard in appearance." He travelled to Boston and purchased a revolver, and upon his return to Franklin, spent long hours in the woods practicing his aim. His behavior alarmed his friends and neighbors, who worried that he might be plotting suicide. Increasingly, he behaved like a stalker. One day, after practicing his aim in the woods, he turned up at the South Franklin school, where Susan was a student. He demanded to see her at the door of the school, but Susan refused to join him.

Jonathon's anger at Susan's rejection was intense, but it was the debaters at the South Franklin Lyceum who drove him over the edge. Meeting in the school house one evening, the Lyceum's members held a debate on whether or not a married man should be ten years older than his wife. Jonathon was invited to argue in favor of the idea. As the *Daily Traveller* put it, "The school house was crowded, and, as was intended, the discussion soon assumed a personal character, and his affairs were alluded to with such freedom as to exasperate him greatly. After this he was frequently joked on the subject, and it is thought that this disregard for his finest feelings caused the deliberate commission of the double crime." The *Daily Traveller* added, in no uncertain terms, "We have the names of those who originated the plan of the discussion, but refrain from publishing them; if the persons have human feelings they will suffer enough with this publicity. Two tombstones will soon be erected, which will be the lasting monuments to their careless and unfeeling conduct."

Not long after the Lyceum discussion, Jonathon stopped Susan in the road and tossed her a note that was later reprinted in the *Daily Traveller*. The letter began:

My dear and beloved one—I take this opportunity of writing to you a few lines to express my feelings in the affair between you and me, hoping you will receive the same feelings for me. Susan, when I think this affair of ours over, and see how it is, and what trouble it has made between us all, it makes me shed many silent tears over it; for peace and harmony together is the beauty of this life, and that this trouble may be done away with is my wish and my prayer. Now when we meet each other, we make no talk together nor see each other. O. this looks awful to me to think It can [be] so But we know that this world is full of trouble on all sides of it—trouble that we need not have if we would only do by each other as we ought.

Jonathon went on to write:

Susan, I suppose you have had a hard time of it with your folks—there is no doubt of that I think and I blame them more than I do you. All I blame you for is for not telling me how it was; but for you to come up and say you never promised to have me, is awful to put up with I tell you. How can you deny this, I ask you? Susan, you are the one I love for all of any one else in this world. You are the one which I want to be united with in this life.

Susan never responded to Jonathon's note, perhaps because of her parents' watchfulness. During the church service, a few days later, Susan's mother left early with her daughter when Jonathon arrived for the service. The following evening, Susan's parents allowed her to attend a party at the house of Nathaniel Hawes, on condition that she ride home with her uncle, Willard Whiting, who was in the neighborhood for a temperance meeting.

Jonathon Wales was also at the party that night. The other party goers noticed that he was in better spirits than he had been for several weeks, but nonetheless, he watched Susan like a hawk. After midnight, Susan left the party with a young man named Ephraim Follett. Jonathon followed them out, crossing a darkened field. The two stepped aside to let him pass, as he came up behind them, but as he approached he drew his revolver and fired a single shot at point-blank range into the right hand side of Susan's head. As Susan went limp against Follett's shoulder, he laid her to the ground and hastened to a nearby house for help. As he ran to the house, Jonathan turned and leaped over a fence, dashing up a hill into the shadows of the woods.

Susan's aunt, by this point, had begun to worry, and set out for Hawes' house to find her niece. Just as she was about to reach the Hawes' house, she had met Susan and Ephraim heading for Susan's house. Relieved, she turned back to her own horse, but was startled moments later by a gunshot. She supposed that the gun had been fired as a joke, but she turned around to investigate. It did not take long to find Susan, and her blood spattered escort. Susan was lifted and carried into the nearest house, where she was surrounded immediately by fellow party goers. Dr. King, the face of Franklin medicine at the time, was called. He arrived soon after the shooting but could do little to remedy Susan's wound. She never regained consciousness and at two a.m. passed away.

At dawn, a small posse of South Franklin men--including Joseph Wadsworth--set out into the woods and swamps. Before the party set out, Jonathon's father, Mr. Wales had been informed. Rather than expressing grief, Wales expressed his desire to find his son dead. A mile from the site of the meadow, in a patch of woods on the side of Bald Hill in Bellingham, the party found Jonathan Wales. His father's prayer had been granted --Jonathan had shot himself in the pit of the stomach. Jonathan's body was soaked in blood; it was said that even his boots were full.

Although the murder-suicide did not directly involve George Wadsworth, he recorded the event in his diary. It seems likely that he would have heard a great deal about the events surrounding the murder, from friends and neighbors, not to mention his brother, who had been a member of the search party. For a few days, Wadsworth crawled with reporters, from far away Boston. In Franklin Center, the news of the murder must have been the talk of the town. According to the *Daily Traveller* the murder was the first to take place in Franklin in a century.

On January 28th, the *Woonsocket Patriot* reported on the funerals held for both Susan and Jonathan. Susan Whiting's funeral was held at the South Franklin Congregational church. The church--little more than a whitewashed neighborhood meetinghouse was filled to overflowing. About 1500 mourners gathered for the funeral, packing the church so tightly that several hundred had to grieve outside. Reverend Thayer, the minister of the South Franklin church, used the funeral as an opportunity to caution parents to respect the happiness of their children. After the service, Susan's body was carried to West Wrentham and placed in the Whiting family's tomb.

Jonathan Wales' funeral was also held at the South Franklin church, with Reverend Thayer presiding. Originally, Mr. Wales had planned to have the funeral at his house, but Jonathan's friends had lobbied for a service at the church. Despite stormy weather, a large crowd gathered at the church. In reconciliation, Susan Whiting's family attended the funeral. The coffin containing Jonathan's body was taken to Bellingham Center, and temporarily interred in a crypt until the spring thaw, when Mr. Wales planned to bury his son in the family plot.

The same day that the two funerals were reported in the *Patriot*, the same newspaper carried statements from the South Franklin Lyceum. The authors of the letter were trying hard to mend the Lyceum's now badly damaged image. "Instead of being willing to sacrifice the feelings of Mr. Wales, for the love of sport, he had the cordial sympathy of the members of the Lyceum, every one of whom was his personal friend, and felt a kindly interest in his behalf," they wrote.

On January 20th, George Wadsworth served as one of the pall-bearers for Susan Whiting's funeral, and the following day, he trudged through the mud on Washington Street to attend Wales' funeral. Joseph Wadsworth was one of the bearers in Wales' funeral.

After witnessing both funerals, George seems to have needed a change of scenery. He left Wadsworth for Boston on January 27th, and changed trains for Ashland once he arrived in the metropolis. He spent a few weeks with his cousins, John and Alvah Metcalf, who operated a box factory, and a cracker factory. For George, perhaps, the time spent grinding grain, shaving wood, and running errands to South Framingham seems to have helped him to get his mind off of the killings.

City Mills, shown in this early postcard, was one of Franklin's most important manufacturing villages until 1869, when it joined parts of Medway, Wrentham, and Walpole to form Norfolk.

One of the earliest images of Franklin Center—now better known as downtown—is this picture taken from Mortimer Blake's 1878 history. The house shown is Dr. Emmons' residence. As Franklin's preacher and librarian for decades, Emmons owned a large estate that later became Dean College.

The wealthy and entrepreneurial Ray family's Elm Farm, seen here in an 1880s panoramic map of the town, was one of the most modern farms in Franklin, and a reflection of the wealth generated by the mills along Mine Brook in Unionville.

Chapter 7:

The Civil War

...before ending the war escorting prisoners. Cook saw more fighting than most and experienced three of the war's fiercest and most decisive battles...

December 24, 1860, the day that South Carolina seceded from the union, George Wadsworth spent six and a half hours repairing shoes, and preparing his sleigh for the winter season. Wadsworth kept himself busy with farm chores—such as spreading manure in his meadow—even as the Civil War began. Surprisingly, his diaries hardly even mention tumultuous events across the nation.

In May 1861, after the Confederacy routed a Union army at Bull Run, Washington realized that it would need more troops. In addition to federal troops under the president's command, Union forces were growing as volunteer militiamen from the north were called up to help. The selectmen of Franklin set aside 3000 dollars for war related expenses, and asked for volunteers to go south. When the call went out, volunteers overfilled Franklin's quota. As the war went on, some soldiers were drafted, but most enlisted voluntarily with local regiments. Departing soldiers were presented with Bibles, at the town hall, and swore to stay sober until war's end. William Makepeace Thayer, a prominent author, temperance advocate, and local resident, may have been behind the sobriety pledge.

The first group of volunteers was organized by a man named Lewis Whitaker, one of three Franklin men who had participated in the anti-slavery struggle known as "Bleeding Kansas." Along with Dr. Amory Hunting (another temperance figure of the 1820s) and Captain Hartford Leonard, Whitaker had traveled to Kansas as armed opponents to slavery. Whitaker returned from Kansas, and ultimately served as an artilleryman guarding the Massachusetts coast, but Dr. Hunting remained in the west, settling in Manhattan, Kansas.

The best source of information about Franklin's Civil War soldiers comes from Franklin High School. In the 2000s, history teacher John Leighton led his students on an extensive research project, uncovering information about 140 of Franklin's 218 Civil War fighters. After almost 150 years, most details are sketchy, but some things are known about these men.

For example, Caleb Ballou (most likely a relative of the prominent Adin Ballou) worked as a farmer in Franklin. He married a woman from Ireland, in 1856, and enlisted as a mounted infantryman. Ballou was captured by the Confederates and shipped to Andersonville prison-- a concentration camp in western Georgia, with so many prisoners that it had become the fifth largest city in the South. Despite extremes of heat and cold, flies, disease and starvation, Ballou survived Andersonville to return to Franklin, although he was permanently disabled.

Owen Wales, unlike Ballou, worked at an industrial job, producing straw bonnets. He served in North Carolina and made it back to Franklin unscathed. By far one of the oldest Franklinites to serve was Norman Hastings, an engineer by trade. When he joined the 45th Regiment he was already forty six years old--the approximate life expectancy of most Americans. Although Hastings' regiment fought in three significant battles, he was able to avoid combat, perhaps as a result of his age. However, Hastings did not make it back to Franklin. On the return journey to Boston, he died of disease on the transport ship.

Franklin men typically joined Massachusetts regiments, but some enlisted with regiments from Connecticut and Rhode Island, when Massachusetts quotas were overfilled. William H. Jackson enlisted with the 15th Connecticut Regiment, Company B, and fought at Antietam and Fredericksburg--Civil War bloodbaths, both. Wesley H. Haslam also enlisted with a Connecticut regiment, the 18th, and participated in the Battle of Winchester. He survived the war and later devoted himself to Franklin's Methodist church. Joseph W. Cook, born in Franklin, joined the 1st Rhode Island Cavalry and fought in the Shenandoah Valley. His cavalry unit later fought at the Second Battle of Bull Run, Fredericksburg and Gettysburg, before ending the war escorting prisoners. Cook saw more fighting than most and experienced three of the war's fiercest and most decisive battles.

A few men even joined the US Navy, such as Samuel Bourne. After returning from blockade duty, he spent the rest of his life quietly, living close to the common. He died in 1932, one of the last surviving Civil War veterans in Franklin.

When the war finally ended in 1865, returning soldiers had acquired a taste for coffee. Regiments brewed huge quantities of coffee, hoping that their soldiers would steer clear of alcohol. Making coffee over an open fire was time consuming, and only made sense for serving dozens of men. Capitalizing on the growing popularity of coffee, Franklin's own James Mason secured the first US patent for a coffee percolator in 1865.

During the war, Massachusetts was a major supplier of food, clothing and weapons for the Union. Franklin produced a wide variety of crops along with manufactured goods. Surprisingly, wild cranberries were one of the town's largest crops, grown in bogs along the streams feeding into the Mill River.

According to agricultural historian Howard Russell, Franklin had one large, 25 acre bog that yielded 1,050 barrels of cranberries in the year 1863. By comparison, the town on Cape Cod with the largest number of cranberry farms --Harwich-- produced only three times as many (at the time, inland marshes were preferred for growing wild cranberries—ultimately domestic varieties took their place, leading to growth in Cape Cod growing).

In addition to its agricultural and industrial output, New England was second to none in higher education, turning out more college graduates (mostly teachers or ministers) than almost any other part of the country. Colleges in New England probably faced a scarcity of new students, as young, well-educated men went south and became officers in the Union army. With an eye to the future, the Universalists set up a committee to create a new college, in 1864.

As the committee solicited contributions of land and money, Stoughton was the first community to reply. Stoughton Universalists were willing to offer 20,000 dollars and a site to build a college. However, Stoughton was outdone by Oliver Dean, in Franklin. Dean was one of the wealthiest and most well respected men in town. He owned Dr. Emmons' former estate (in Franklin Center), and offered the Universalists 60,000 dollars and nine acres. The committee quickly accepted Dean's princely contribution, although a separate site in Medford was also chosen to build a theological school to train ministers.*

Trustees were appointed and a charter was secured, and the ground breaking took place in 1866. In 1867, the cornerstone was laid. The economic problems that followed the Civil War raised the cost of building materials and workers, so that Oliver Dean eventually paid out 75,000 dollars for construction. The building was completed in 1868 and Dean Academy was born. The newly finished school was very modern, equipped with brand new furniture and a 'gas apparatus,' for lighting. The new school was a source of immense pride for the local Universalist congregation. Out of all the towns in Massachusetts, many with larger numbers of Universalists than Franklin, their town had been given a great distinction.

As the Universalists completed a college, and added a parish school, the town moved to expand its own schools. In 1868, a high school was set

*Franklin was originally considered as a location for Tufts University, another Universalist college, and the home of the Crane Theological School, long used to train Universalist ministers.

up with a first class of 22 students. An 1879 map indicates that the high school was held along with a grammar (middle), and elementary school in the Red Brick School.

At the end of the 1860s, Franklin lost one its most valuable villages to the new town of Norfolk. In the present day, City Mills is a historic village within Norfolk, marked by a red-painted mill building, brambles, and a field for horses located next to a pond, only a short distance from Acorn Animal Hospital and the Adirondack Club. The village of City Mills had been an important settlement within Franklin since its incorporation. The mills were profitable and its location on one of the two main roads leading out of town had brought commerce to the area. Because of its strategic location, City Mills had even been home to the original town post office.

On October 18, 1869, residents of sparsely populated North Wrentham, an area that had already secured a measure of autonomy from the town, petitioned the Massachusetts General Court to separate from Wrentham and become a new town. The movement for a new town was not limited to North Wrentham. Voters from northeast Franklin (City Mills), southeast Medway, and western Walpole all backed the petition. As with Wrentham's second precinct a few generations earlier, residents in northeastern Franklin were tired of traveling to and from the center of town to attend church and municipal meetings.

When the petition was presented to the General Court, its members agreed that the petition's creators had every justification for wanting their own town. The proposed name for the town – shared with the county from which it sprang -- was Norfolk -- literally, the north people. The General Court decided to grant their wish and drew up plans to break off parts of each of the four towns. The new town of Norfolk would have a population of 1,124. Out of that number, 850 were Wrenthamites, 234 were Franklinites, and only 40 were from Medway and Walpole. 1,100 acres of Franklin land changed hands, along with 39 houses. It was a serious financial loss for Franklin.

Following the land cession, City Mills became one of the main sources of Norfolk tax revenue. Although its inhabitants had decided to join the new town, City Mills remained an industrial colony of Franklin for more than a decade. The mill owners lived in Franklin, and companies such as the City Mills Company were based in Franklin. The name lived on in Franklin with one of the town schools referred to as City Mills as late as 1883.

Over time, Franklin's influence in City Mills began to fade. Mills changed hands and new industries came to the area, and Franklin became more and more disinvested in its former property.

Part II:
From Village to Town

Franklin's main rail station around the turn of the 20th century, note the gas lamp for illuminating the station and the sign on the hill. The introduction of the railroad during the 1840s brought the first Catholics to town and sped up local industrialization. Note the once "famous" Franklin sign on the right, composed of painted stones. (Courtesy of Franklin Public Library)

Chapter 8:

The 1870s

...The earliest riser looked out upon the streets fairly glorious with flags and every species of elegant decoration which could be devised...

In the early 1870s, the country was hit by a financial panic that left many Americans in poverty. Although some New Englanders must have felt the impact of US financial problems, New England was well situated to weather the storm. Thousands of New England farmers had joined the army during the Civil War and many had never returned, leaving rural areas and farms permanently understaffed. But in the cities and towns, mills were booming, staffed by new Irish immigrants, who churned out the goods needed to rebuild the war ravaged country.

To cash in on the demand for all kinds of different goods, dams were built on even the tiniest streams, and mills crowded in to take advantage of running water to power their operations. Set far back from Lincoln Street, along tiny Shepard's Brook, was a box factory, flanked with worker's housing and a cotton mill. Along the Charles River, houses had sprung up to hold the overflow of laborers from Medway's mills, while elsewhere on Lincoln Street, interspersed with farms were a marble shop and a fruit and vegetable cannery. Elbowed out by the demand for textiles (and the general lack of trees in town) saw mills had virtually disappeared. One did continue on Washington Street, however, powered by water from Dix Brook, producing planks for a boat shop across the street. At the boat shop, carpenters labored every day of the week except Sunday, to build rowboats for coastal sale.

Out of all Franklin industries, straw hats were the most lucrative. Straw hat factories produced hundreds of thousands of hats annually, with sale value totaling more than a million dollars.

To transport new products, local entrepreneurs spent heavily to expand railroads. A line from Franklin to Adamsdale (in Bristol County) was built across northern Rhode Island, with stops in Cumberland. Edgar Ray, a member of the powerful Ray family became the president of the Milford, Franklin & Providence Railroad in 1868 (he later became known as the "electric rail king of Rhode Island").

Everyone in Franklin was busy, but managed to find time to attend church, take part in events, and join a wave of new fraternal organizations appearing in town. A building boom took place as different congregations rushed to build bigger and better churches. The Universalists, so pleased with the spectacle of Dean Academy, wanted a church to match. It would not look right, if an impressive school like

Dean was flanked by a small church. In June, 1874, the Universalists abandoned their church and moved it down School Street for use by the Baptists. The Baptists were not a large group in Franklin in the 1870s, but the former Universalist church suited them perfectly as far as size.

In place of the old church, the Universalists hurried to put up the Grace Church. The new church cost the congregation a huge sum, but the end result was described by Mortimer Blake as, "...One of the most beautiful and perfectly appointed houses of worship to be found in any town in New England." The new church and an enthusiastic minister named Reverend Chambre transformed the Universalists from a relatively minor local religious group into one of the largest congregations in town. Now the Universalist church complemented the size and architecture of Dean Academy.

Even for a large religious community, it is difficult to come up with large sums of money almost overnight. Initial work on the Dean Academy was paid for by Oliver Dean, but when the college burnt down in 1872, the Universalists needed to come up with the money to rebuild the school while simultaneously building the Grace church. Remarkably, the Universalists accomplished both goals in record time, rebuilding Dean Academy by 1874. The college started out small, accepting both men and women up until 1877, and then briefly became a women's only college for two years.

The growing Irish-Catholic community moved out of the town hall in 1871, and into the old Congregationalist church at the northern end of the common, a site they still occupy more than 130 years later.

Eager to take advantage of the money pouring into Franklin, Reverend Cushing, a Methodist student from Boston came to Franklin and pushed forward a Methodist church and a 'revival.' Continuing construction even during the winter, a church was finished by March, 1873. Two hundred people converted to Methodism, swelling the community's ranks and helping them to afford construction.

Smaller numbers of other faiths did exist in Franklin. Members of the New Jerusalem Church, also known as Swedenborgians (after the founding ideas of a man named Swedenborg) met in a house for weekly services. A few aging utopians lived in Franklin, dreaming up a better world. One of them was Adin Ballou, a Unitarian preacher who lived on East Central Street. Earlier in life (during the 1840s) Ballou founded Hopedale as a utopian community. The utopia did not work out right, and Ballou subsequently retired to Franklin, living a quiet life except for the visits of great men such as William Lloyd Garrison.

The same ideals that drove local groups to finance bigger and better churches, inspired non-religious, fraternal groups to move into the area for the first time. The International Order of Odd Fellows set up a lodge in 1878, along with groups such as the Freemasons.

Franklin's ever increasing prosperity was not for everyone, and the town poor farm had 12 inhabitants by Blake's count at the end of the 1870s, although the number was always fluctuating. The oldest was 81, the youngest 24, but most were in their sixties and seventies. These paupers lived at the poor farm on the shore of Uncas Pond. The first poor farm had burned down in 1868, and was rebuilt by the town at a slightly different location. These unfortunate individuals worked full time at the poor farm raising the money to pay for their room and board.

In 1876, the year of the national bicentennial, the town fathers decided that it was time to start planning a celebration of Franklin's 100th anniversary. They convinced Reverend Mortimer Blake (former head of the Red Brick school) to write a history of the town. He consented, researching and printing *A History of the Town of Franklin, Mass.; From its Settlement to the Completion of its First Century*. Unlike the wealth of charlatan historians who printed 'history' in the 19th century, Blake put a lot of effort into his book, inquiring with the older inhabitants of the town about unusual details, and old events.

Blake himself had plenty of experience with Franklin's past, having grown up in town. As a child, he read many of Benjamin Franklin's books and proved a precocious learner, teaching himself Latin by age 10 and Hebrew as a teenager. After attending a private academy in Medway, Blake went to Amherst College, and afterwards worked as a school teacher and a minister.

On June 12, 1878 came the culmination of two years of planning and Blake's extensive research as Franklin celebrated Centennial Day. The celebration cost the town 500 dollars, but it seems to have gotten full value for the money. The committee that had organized the celebration included some town notables such as James P. Ray and the Reverend Chambre (who had recently built the Methodist church).

J.M. Stewart, the owner and editor of the *Franklin Register* (Franklin's earliest newspaper, started in 1872) was caught up in the excitement of the centennial and wrote, "At 6 o'clock on the morning of 12th of June, 1878, the jubilant bells and the crashing and growling voices of the cannon announced that the ceremonies of the day were about to commence. The earliest riser looked out upon the streets fairly glorious with flags and every species of elegant decoration which could be devised..."

"At a very early hour the streets began to show throngs of people, and the arrivals from the cities and neighboring towns rapidly swelled the crowds until it was estimated that 10,000 perhaps more, people were abroad to celebrate the grand occasion. At 10 o'clock came the

Governor of the State [(Alexander H. Rice, a Republican)] and his staff, Lieutenant-Governor, Secretary of State, and the Executive Council, M.P Wilder, Manager Clark and other officials from the New York and New England Railroad, and other distinguished guests."

In preparation for the event, some Franklin women created the first town museum. "The museum of antiquities, to which allusion has been made, was in the capacious chapel in the rear of Congregational church. Nearly a thousand people visited it during the day, and it was opened, at a small entrance fee, for two succeeding days." Although it was only temporary, the Congregational ladies guild put a great deal of effort into assembling it. The collection, when the museum opened, included, "Bibles and books of all ages, from an illuminated Roman missal of 1485, on vellum...[to] a series of manuscript sermons by the Wrentham and Franklin pastors..."

Other items included, "...An hour glass, 180 years old....a brass milk-pan used by British soldiers in Boston...an old brass clock, six feet high...China sets, platters, etc." In truth, the collection included just about everything from buckskin breaches to an 'old-time kitchen,' Dr. Emmons' tri-corner hat to the bell, supposedly worn by the first cow in Franklin.

The day began with a parade, described in great detail by Blake. Leading the procession, a unit of cavalry marched through town, followed by a cornet band from Woonsocket, and the fire department. Many ordinary people took part in the parade as well. Members of the local chapter of the Grand Army of the Republic (an organization of Union veterans) marched along with Franklin school children, a band from Medway, and the Ancient Order of Hibernians (an Irish fraternal organization) Franklin and Milford lodges. Of course, no one wanted to exclude Governor Rice and his staff who had left Boston at an early hour to attend, so the politicians were allowed to join the parade.

The parade offered Franklin businessmen a chance to advertise themselves free of charge. The Trowbridge piano company had several wagons loaded with musical instruments, while the Rays displayed their felt products, and a series of butchers, wheelwrights, carpenters, cobblers and grocers displayed their products. One member of the Ray family loaded a wagon with antique furniture and equipped it with some volunteer actors. As the wagon made its way across town, one young woman volunteer operated a spinning wheel, trying to recreate a scene from the time of the American Revolution. S.W. Thayer, a shoe maker displayed boots and shoes, including, as a gimmick, a shoe made for the largest foot at the next centennial. Unfortunately, this enormous shoe appears to have been lost long before the 1978 bicentennial rolled around.

After the parade came to an end, Edwin Trowbridge, owner of a piano manufacturing company, led a choir in singing. No centennial celebration would be complete without a Biblical lesson thrown in and Reverend Thayer read from the Bible and led the town in prayer. After the prayer, Reverend Mortimer Blake took center stage.

At the start of his speech, Blake explained the modest origins of his history and the participation of townspeople in its completion. "I must preface, however, that it is with great timidity I consented to be the spokesman...this hour. Living so far and so long from the sources of information, and crowded with the never-finished work of my vocation, it has only been by short visits and broken explorations that I have searched records to collate the story of this town's past. If the results seem meager, please charge it—not to want of interest in the seeking, but the lack of time and material. And, had it not been for the zealous co-operation of your committee in charge of this celebration, and of other interested citizens, and the cordial responses of the town clerks into whose records the sources of our town history run back, and of Wrentham in particular, the present address would still be meager."

His 'meager' address lasted for an hour and 20 minutes. "I have simply culled a few of the taller stalks from the harvest-field of a hundred years, to make a boquet [sic] for your centennial table to-day. It is a specimen only out of the years from which others might have gathered a much richer handful. But to me the culling has been among familiar acres, and the work has been a labor of love. As such, I beg to lay it before you to-day, with the hope that you will excuse the omission of your favorite flowers, and accept it as my offering to the old town which has always rendered me far more honor than I feel myself to be worthy of."

With the speechifying and parading done for the day, celebratory townspeople and notable guests headed for the common, where a pavilion had been set up. Only those with tickets were allowed in, but 1200 people were still able to enjoy the centennial supper. "It was not long," writes Mortimer Blake, "Before every seat was occupied, and a vigorous dental activity prevailed for half an hour. It is not possible to report all the good things said at the table. The programme [sic] of speeches intended could not be fully carried out for want of time, even if a sudden shower had not delayed the exercises."

While Franklin maintained some traditions, such as a produce market on the common, other things had changed dramatically. One hundred twenty seven of the town's oldest resident (between 60 and 92 years old) had witnessed tremendous changes since the 1700s. The town had been transformed before their eyes from an agricultural backwater to a major manufacturing center—complete with factories and railroads. By the 1870s, many old families such as the Mann family had already left town. Many of New England's early families had opted to pursue a new life in the west, setting up farms in places such as Wisconsin and Kansas that dwarfed Massachusetts in size. For probably the first time, Franklinites lived from coast to coast. The tiny frontier outpost had become an established town, sending forth its own to populate newer parts of the growing nation.

The Churches

Town Hall Franklin Mass
—1890—

Franklin's town hall, built in 1842 and serving up until the late 20th century was used as a church by many of Franklin's smaller religious groups such as the Catholics and the Methodists during the 1800s.

One of the town's oldest surviving churches, the Methodist church was built in the 1850s.

Built in the 1870s to match the grandeur of Dean Academy, Grace Universalist church was finally torn down in the '60s to make way for a new college library.

Congregational Church, FRANKLIN, Mass.

Overlooking the common, the Congregational church has had a long and varied existence. Today it is the Federated church, serving the combined Baptist and Congregationalist communities.

Originally the Universalist church, the Baptists used the building on School Street until its steeple collapsed in the hurricane of 1938. After that the Baptists moved in with the Congregationalists to form the Federated church.

St. Mary's church acquired the old Congregationalist church by the common in the 1870s and used the building until the 1890s.

Subsequently, until it was gutted by fire in the early '20s, Franklin Catholics relied on a brick church building for their growing community.

ST. MARY'S CHURCH, FRANKLIN, MASS.   264

The current St. Mary's Church was built in 1923, completed rapidly with donated money, after the previous church was destroyed by flames.

Chapter 9:

The 1880s—A Local Golden Age

...Congressman Edward Burnett...insisted, for the benefit of the skeptical audience, that unlike other politicians, he did not try to buy farmers' votes by bribing them with cheap turnip seeds...

The industrial boom of the 1870s sped up in the 1880s, without any serious economic hiccups to slow growth. The Ray family, slowly gathering wealth since the 1840s had enough money in the bank to live an extremely prosperous lifestyle, while giving back to the community. Rays were trustees or directors of many town businesses and organizations, including the Milford, Franklin & Providence Railroad and the Franklin Sugar Beet Company.

The railroad, a local venture on the part of Edgar K. Ray, was chartered in 1882 and began running trains in 1883. The railroad never amounted to much, although it did carry freight and passengers between Franklin, Milford, Bellingham, and Providence, under contract with larger companies. Ultimately, the expense of managing a roundhouse in the center of Franklin, and caring for tracks, proved too great for the tiny company and it was bought out by the New York & New Haven Rail Road in 1898.

Edgar Ray also guided another small startup, the Franklin Sugar Beet Company. Even today, a short street off of Union Street bears the name Sugar Beet Road. The name seems unusual, but stems from Franklin's brief stint in the sugar business. At one point in the early 1880s, several businessmen decided to build a refinery close to the railroad tracks, right off of Union Street. The refinery would process starchy sugar beets, grown by local farmers into a lucrative finished product—granulated sugar. The refinery was built, and for a short while produced sugar, but local farmers were unable to keep up with demand.*

New business ventures were easier to start thanks to banks such as Dean Cooperative, which opened its door in 1889. Individuals could buy an infinite number of one dollar shares in the bank, and earn interest on each tiny investment.

By the 1880s, with new mills in need of protection against fire, the town invested in two horse drawn fire engines (one for Unionville and its mills). A significant focus of the town's activities was maintaining

The Franklin Historical Commission retains a small sample of original sugar from the refinery.

the community's 18 school houses (the count in 1883, down from 21 the year before). The number of children attending school had risen with new arrivals from Ireland, Italy, and elsewhere in Europe. As adults went to work in the felt mills and straw shops, children needed to be educated. Teachers taught a few key subjects, such as geography, history, reading, writing and arithmetic. In addition, the School Committee prided themselves on their music and hygiene programs (in which students learned about the dangers of alcohol, and the benefits of cleanliness).

At the same time, the police were cracking down on illegal drinking establishments in town. Special officer Aaron Morse was hired in 1886 to catch saloonkeepers who failed to pay proper taxes on their beverage sales. To catch people selling 'under the counter,' Morse turned to the courts and procured an astonishing 68 warrants in a single year. Many small saloons operated out of people's homes, and Morse caught many violators. For those caught, penalties could be stiff.

In the town report, Morse wrote that, "On July 16th [1887], Officer Nickerson and myself procured a search warrant for the premises occupied by Phillip McParland on Cottage Street. On arriving at this saloon we found everything to all appearances as usual, and spent some time in looking the establishment over. We found, before we closed our search, a wooden tank secreted between the plastering and the boarding on the outside of the building, which held about four gallons of whiskey. This tank was furnished with a rubber tube extending from the bottom through which the liquor was drawn." McParland was arrested, fined fifty dollars, and sentenced to three months of hard labor in Dedham. Although he met great success in stopping small violators, Morse was annoyed by his inability to catch up with the suppliers of the under the counter alcohol trade. The suppliers were from Milford and delivered weak alcoholic beverages to the town during the day and hard liquor under the cover of nightfall.

With the clampdown on liquor sales, some local druggists and doctors (selling tax-free hard liquor with the protection of their licenses) got caught up in embarrassing run-ins with the law. But if anything, the case of Charles and Joseph Yale, a druggist and dentist respectively, proves that alcohol was only the tip of the iceberg. In January 1884, the brothers were arrested and charged with attempted rape. Allegedly, on January 15, 1884, Charles had tried to rape a young Swedish immigrant to Boston, who was staying in Franklin. According to Flossa Burgerson, the woman in question, the dentist's brother had pitched in, at one point threatening to use his array of chloroform, ether, and tools, to knock her out and pull out all of her teeth. The scandal galvanized local opinion against the two professionals, although Joseph Yale's reputation was already tarnished by a previous conviction for illegally selling rum.

In an unrelated incident in Wrentham, a group of pedestrians discovered the skeleton of an Attleboro woman, several years missing, in the bushes along a main road. Such incidents make it clear that even during boom times such as 1880s crime was never far out of sight.

Politically, Franklin and all its neighbors were fiercely Republican towns. The 1886 gubernatorial election gives an interesting idea of the breakdown of parties locally. Both Democrats and Republicans held local conventions in Franklin, often at the town hall, with delegates invited from Wrentham, Foxboro and Medway. One of the Democratic delegates from Medway was a member of the Knights of Labor, an early labor organization.

At the beginning of November, 1886, the election was held on a cloudless day. Of the 454 voters in Franklin, none expressed any concern about the short hours for which the polls were open--10:00 in the morning until 3:00 in the afternoon. Two hundred fourteen voters chose the Republican ticket, 147 chose the Democratic one, and 47 voted for the Prohibitionist Party, a group dedicated to the outlawing of alcohol.

Even though the Democrats lost in Franklin, they could still celebrate Christmas and the New Year attending the Knights of Labor ball in Medway. Politics was a strange mix of mudslinging and festivity. Responding to a Republican rally at the Morse Opera House in 1888, the Democrats hired a drum corps and had a torchlight parade through town, ending with a speech by Congressman Edward Burnett from Southboro, Massachusetts. Burnett insisted, for the benefit of the skeptical audience, that unlike other politicians, he did not try to buy farmers' votes by bribing them with cheap turnip seeds.

Franklin's politics may have been somewhat divided, but everyone was ready to rally around the local militia battalion. The militia had grown since the 1820s to include more units and more men who were on call in case of a state or national crisis. The men voted for their officers, picking a major, quartermaster, adjutant, color bearer, captains, lieutenants and sergeants each year, and held frequent parades down Main Street to the railroad tracks. Usually the officers were prominent local men.

Beyond simply militia involvement, participating in Franklin's rich social life was a full time occupation. An involved citizen could join any number of men's clubs, women's auxiliaries, agricultural and business organizations, or church groups. Life could be hectic, but these Franklinites knew how to set aside time for friends, family, and the community without giving up on their day jobs.

The fraternal organizations with lodges set up in 1870s had taken great strides toward enlisting new members and establishing themselves, and were even beginning to add auxiliaries for the wives and daughters of the members. For example, the men of the International Order of Odd Fellows were joined by Lodge 66 of the Rebekahs, the women's branch of the I.O.O.F. Rebekah members first appeared at I.O.O.F. lodge in 1882 (although not officially until 1888).

A different fraternal organization, similar to the Masons, Rebekahs, and Odd Fellows, opened a lodge in Franklin on October 31, 1887. The National Grange was founded as a fraternal organization for farmers in 1867, but it took another twenty years to reach Franklin. Although the Odd Fellows and Masons had lofty goals, the National Grange was often the most successful organization when it came time to putting its ideas into action. The Grange, which championed the cause of farmers and rural residents, helped bring postal services to rural areas, saving farmers long trips that took them away from their farms and their work. Before the Social Security system was set up, the National Grange also helped to provide insurance and social benefits for farmers and small businessmen. For Franklin farmers, National Grange membership was a step up.

During the summer, a select few of Franklin athletes competed on the baseball diamond with other towns and villages. Local baseball teams were enormously popular in the 1880s. The most popular team in Franklin was the Dean Academy team, aptly named the Deans. There was a fierce rivalry between the Deans and the towns of Norwood and Milford, along with the Caryvilles (you can guess where they hailed from). Most Franklinites rooted for the Deans, but in the north of town, the Caryvilles were the most popular team.

Fortunately for Franklin, the same prosperity that helped to make baseball so popular helped different groups and even the town at large, to weather a few catastrophic events at the end of the decade. In 1887, the Universalist community was hard hit when their expensive church, the pride and joy of the congregation, burned to the ground and needed to be rebuilt from the ground up. Once again, the Universalists banded together, plunging into construction. The replacement church was completed in a year.

Eleven days into March, 1888, Franklin and the rest of the east coast was hammered by the worst blizzard in two centuries. The Great Blizzard of 1888, as it became known, dropped an *average* of four feet of snow on Franklin, although windblown drifts were much higher.

Later in the year, after all the snow had melted, a panoramic map of Franklin was created. Panoramic maps were very popular in 19th century America, offering a bird's eye view in the absence of aerial photographs, giving people a new perspective on the town. Prints of the original 1888 panoramic map hang in most schools and municipal buildings today, but a quick glance does not always reveal the craftsmanship that went into its creation. On close examination, one can spot incredible detail in the garden of the Ray family mansion and even a staircase in the Ray Block in the center of town. The map gives an idea of downtown Franklin's geographic concentration. The map covers only the center of the town, and around the edges of the map are large fields and woods. The map shows only a few square miles--the rest of the town during the 1880s was largely empty (except for villages)— and more heavily populated by livestock than people.

Even within the center of town, the number of mills and factories depicted is incredible. More than half a dozen were clustered into the area shown on the map. The high level of detail in the map, gives a glimpse into the town as it was almost 125 years, and makes us wonder, what a visitor would see.

As the New York & New England trains rolls into Franklin Center from the east, under a cloud of smoke, it passes the immense Snow Bassett straw works, a four-story monstrosity pouring smoke into the sky, on one side of the tracks. On the other side of the car, a small roundhouse and some houses drop out of sight as the train comes to a stop. Back of the platform are a station and a depot side by side, with a flight of stairs leading up to Main Street.

Main Street is the real center of town. On one side of the street, are an apothecary, a dry goods store and a millinery shop to name a few, with the Metcalf lumber mill in the back alley. Opposite (roughly where the present day post office and Dean Bank are located) is Ray's Block—a building housing an attorney, a general store, the post office, and the library.

Walking up Main Street, a visitor would pass a doctor's office and two mansions—the result of Franklin's growing wealth—opposite Dean Academy. Where the Franklin Public Library is located today was a house and paddock. Across the road (currently E. Ross Anderson Library) is the Grace Universalist church. The Universalists have to put up with the racket from a mill across School Street from the church. The Baptists, with their church downhill along School Street have it little better, sharing the street with a livery stable, the high school (right next door) and the Thayer mill at the corner.

Further along Main Street, the Congregationalist church and the Catholic church are better situated around the common in a largely residential part of town. It is hard to say for sure which part of the Center is busiest. At times, Central Street and Main Street, with their churches, grocery stores, close by mills, and the town hall are busiest.

However, during the day, most people in the Center work in the mills along Union Street by the railroad tracks. Worker housing lines Cottage Street abutting the tracks, while homeowners in search of larger yards own the houses down Peck and Washington Street. Children head to the twin Nason Street schools during the day, while their parents work at eight different mills at the junction of Cottage and Union Street. With so many mills in the area, their machinery powered by coal-fueled steam engines, the neighborhood is usually a sooty place, made even worse whenever a train stops to load or unload. The tracks split, with the NY & NE heading southeast towards Wadsworth, while the Milford, Franklin & Providence branches off to the west toward Beaver Pond.

Factories extend away from Franklin Center into the woods around Beaver Pond. The pond is tapped by the Franklin Water Company, a new company as of 1887, with a pump house across the tracks from the rubber works—another infamous local polluter. The 1888 map provides a unique and very detailed glimpse into the downtown Franklin of almost 125 years ago. It is a moment in time that captures the vitality of a town full of energy and change.

A Village Transformed

Dean Academy, launched in 1865, was rebuilt in the 1870s following a fire. The newer building (above) remains the center of campus today. The building's bell tower was destroyed by the 1938 hurricane and replaced with a radio antenna.

The Metcalf Block and Music Hall was a major center for shops along Main Street during the 1880s.

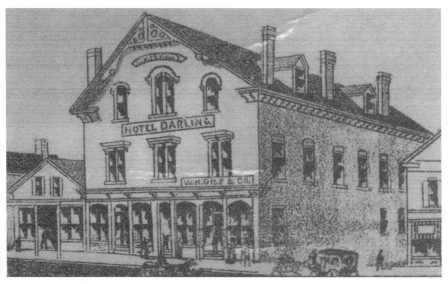

Long before the Holiday Inn opened in Franklin, Hotel Darling offered visitors a place to stay the night.

Waitts Felting Mill was smaller than many mills, located close to the tracks in Franklin Center. However, at a time when other mills focused on straw products, Waitts was already producing non-woven textiles—such as felt—starting a new trend in local manufacturing that persists to this day in the operations at Clark Cutler & McDermott.

Snow, Bassett, & Company's mill in downtown (later known as the Golding mill, and Thomason Press) was one of the largest mills in the 1880s. The mill specialized in straw products, particularly straw hats.

The twin Main Street residences of James and Joseph Ray, two of Franklin's wealthiest men, were the products of the town's wealth during the boom years of 1870s, and the 'Gilded Age' of the 1880s.

Chapter 10:

The 1890s

...Mrs. E.P. Blackmer was the person who had discovered the gold seam 15 years earlier...

For some reason, everyone in the 20th century looked back on the 1890s nostalgically. In fact, the 1890s were hardly as good a time for average people as the 1880s. Early in the decade, a crippled economy led to widespread poverty and layoffs. As in the 1870s, Franklin was fairly well situated to weather the poor economy, but even prosperous places felt its effect.

Many characteristics of the 1880s remained the same. The town government stayed small, employing people on a part time basis to supply wood and coal for town buildings and to teach. The town paid six fire wardens to watch the woods during the summer for brush fires, three fence viewers to protect crops from roaming livestock, an oil inspector to protect consumer from poor quality kerosene, and several 'field drivers,' catching stray animals. The Franklin Police Department remained small and the special liquor officer was often busier than his regular counterparts, hauling liquor violators into court. Two night officers made sure that all was well after hours and a truant officer hunted for students who skipped school. He caught two boys, 'playing hookie' and sent them to reform school in Walpole.

Falling under the jurisdiction of the oil inspector were the Bullukian family and their oil company. An Armenian immigrant success story, Harry Bullukian and his sons set up a small business in 1898. The three of them worked hard to keep their company afloat, strengthening their muscles shoveling coal off of rail cars and delivering large oil drums door to door. In spite of its small beginnings the Bullukian oil company became very successful and still exists today.

A few new service organizations moved into town, including the Order of the Eastern Star in 1894, and a local startup, the Alden Club, in 1892. For citizens aspiring to prominence, the Franklin Country Club was a sensible organization to pick. At the end of 1899, 21 people from Franklin gathered at the house of Adelbert Thayer to buy 150 acres of land for development into the Country Club. The Country Club had many members who were also involved with Franklin Business Association, a group known for its philanthropy, and for its work benefiting the local economy, most importantly attracting the Golding Mfg. Co. to set up a factory.

The Rays remained as prominent as ever, with one member of the family appointed to the state Grand Lodge of the I.O.O.F. Another member of the Ray family was mourned by Franklinites following his death in 1898, of a heart attack, at age 54. William F. Ray had lived larger than life in their eyes, graduating the youngest in his class at Brown University, and quickly becoming the manager of three mills (he also organized the Norfolk Woolen Company), and three banks, all while serving as a selectman, head of the school committee, state representative, and state senator.

In the 1890s, the town began to shift away from straw hat production to the new non-woven industry. Non-wovens include felt and other textiles made without weaving. A few felting mills such as Waite's produced felt locally during the 1880s, but new producers entered the field as better technology appeared.

Franklin's wealth came from textiles, and for a short time in 1898, from the ground. On November 17, the *Boston Post* reported on a sensational "gold rush" in Franklin.* "There is but one topic here today," wrote the correspondent. "It is gold on every tongue and from present indications, it bids fair to be more than the usual nine days' wonder. Although no Klondike boom** has struck the town yet, Franklin calmly awaits and half expects it."

The correspondent was not exaggerating, as the article went on to explain: "The hotel and restaurant keepers are seriously thinking of building additions and sending to Boston for an extra supply of canned goods. Sign painters confidently expect large increases in orders. They are practising [sic] on such signs as 'Come to the Miners' Rest,' 'Gold Dust Accepted Here,' 'The Only Place to Get Real Klondike** Beef Stews,' 'Hamburg Steak a la Dawson and Franklin.'"

"The trains to Franklin—passenger and freight—were full of passengers coming to prospect and invest in gold. In the words of the correspondent, "It was a woman who created all this excitement, and also discovered the gold vein, and here is a curious thing, for it disproves the time-honored proverb that a woman cannot keep a secret."

Mrs. E.P. Blackmer was the person who had discovered the gold seam 15 years earlier. She had kept the find to herself, telling no one— not even her husband and closest friends. The vein of quartz and gold ran in a low ledge from Alpine Street to Fales Street. Blackmer spent

It turns out Franklin wasn't alone, several gold mines were started in Wrentham during the 1800s.

**Referring to the massive 1897 Klondike gold rush in Alaska and the Canadian Yukon.*

months buying up her neighbor's land along the seam, before revealing the discovery. Blackmer's father was a surveyor, and she had known about the gold from a young age, but only confirmed her belief when Jerome Prince, a mining expert from Milford, arrived in town with a machine for finding gold. She recruited Prince, and made him a partner in the find.

As word got around, men, women and children began buying up hatchets and hammers from all of the local hardware stores, and breaking off chunks of rock where it came to the surface on private property, or along Fales Street. According to the correspondent, people snuck around town with pockets bulging with rock, while other groups lit up Fales Street throughout the night with lamps as they carried off rock from the roadside. What exactly became of Franklin's gold rush is unclear, with interest probably petering out.

The militia, that had spent so many years drilling on weekends, finally had a taste of war in 1898. After decades of rebellion and unrest in Cuba, America, spurred on by sensationalist newspapers, had plunged into a war with Spain to protect its interests in the Caribbean. When the US went to war with Spain, a few young Franklin men packed their bags and donned uniforms better suited for the Arctic than for the tropics. It was the first time since the Civil War that Franklin men had marched away to fight and the first time that Franklin men are known to have participated in a war on foreign soil. It was a brief war and most of the casualties were as a result of yellow fever and intestinal illnesses rather than bullets. Nonetheless, Franklin's 35 warriors returned wearing invisible laurels on their heads--they were heroes for a new generation, too young to remember the Civil War and its aftermath. And they returned with the 20th century and all its promise fast approaching.

Horace Mann High School, built 1898, served until the mid-'20s. Located at the corner of Emmons Street, the building was later remodeled as an elementary school and then a town hall. It is now used by the Recreation Department.

The current Davis Thayer school opened its doors as the high school in 1925, serving until 1962 when a new high school (the current Horace Mann middle school) was built on Oak Street.

As the name suggests, the Ray School was a gift of the Ray family, much like the Joseph Ray Memorial Library. It was located on School St.

In 1917, when this photo was taken, the Unionville school was one of only two district schools still heated with wood stoves. The school was very primitive and had no running water to speak of, and nothing besides outhouses for students.

The Arlington Street School, serving Franklin's younger students on the edge of the downtown, closely resembles the twin Nason Street elementary schools that existed around the turn of the 20th century.

The Theron Metcalf School, one of several modern brick schools in town when photographed in 1917. It served a large immigrant neighborhood in the downtown. Today, the building is used for elder housing.

The Nason Street school, used as a grammar (middle) school in 1917, was probably cooler during the warm months of the year than other schools thanks to an abundance of shade trees.

The wooden Thayer School was not as modern as some, and so served as one of the town's elementary schools.

This rare, and never before published image from *A Sanitary Survey of Franklin* shows children playing at what appears to be the Metcalf school.

The Red Brick school claims the title of oldest operational one-room school in the country, with classes held continuously from 1835 to 2000. During the 1870s, the building housed the high school, as well as a grammar and primary school.

Chapter 11:

A New Century

...To coincide with the bicentennial event, the children's department of the Ray Memorial Library was unveiled with 1500 books... purchased with money deposited in 1848 by 16 year old Joseph G. Ray...

The turn of the 20th century brought more than a few positive changes to Franklin. Wealthy individuals who had amassed fortunes in the 1880s were able to fund projects around the downtown. A bronze plaque with the full text of the Gettysburg Address was mounted on a boulder, while a statue went up to commemorate Franklin volunteers and some of the bloodier battles--for example, Antietam-- in which they had fought. In 1903, the masonry gazebo was erected in the center of the common. The Civil War monument was donated by a man named Frederick Atwood Newell, who subsequently moved to Attleboro. The gazebo was also donated--a landmark contributed by the Hayward family. The brass plaque of the Gettysburg Address, though, was funded by the Grand Army of the Republic.

At the corner of School Street and Main Street, opposite the Grace church, a new home for Franklin's public library was built between 1901 and 1904. Joseph Gordon Ray, patriarch of the Ray family, was born in Mendon in 1831. In 1854, he married a woman named Emily Rockwood. Together, they enjoyed married life until his death in 1900. Soon after he passed away, his two daughters--Annie Ray Thayer and Lydia Ray Peirce decided to donate the present library building to the town. The building was intended to enshrine the memory of their late father and as a result, it was named the Ray Memorial Library.

Ray's two daughters spared no expense to make the building unique--a piece of art. They hired two prominent painters to paint the scenes in the front hall, the reading room, and the reference room. The large friezes in the present day reference room and in the front entrance hall were painted by an Italian artist named Tommaso Juglaris. Born in Turin, Italy in 1844, Juglaris studied with some of Italy's finest artists in Turin before immigrating to the United States in 1880.

At the time the Ray Memorial Library was built, Juglaris was at the height of his fame, teaching classes in Boston to the world's best aspiring artists. He had even been decorated by the King of Italy. The friezes that he was hired to paint in Franklin depicted elements of Greek mythology. One series shows the 'Greek Hours.' The Hours included

Pleasure, Morning, Evening, Sleep and Labor. Another series of friezes depicted a Grecian festival. Juglaris created the majority of the paintings at the Ray Memorial Library, a smaller number, such as a painting of a camel crossing the desert, were painted by a Boston-born artist named H.H. Gallison, who was well known in the city. The library was constructed of Milford granite, the same stone used for the Boston Public Library.

The town held a large celebration for the bicentennial of Benjamin Franklin's birth, on January 17, 1906. The festival included the reading of an original poem about Benjamin Franklin's life, xylophone solos, and lofty speeches given by notables such as former Massachusetts governor John Bates and Professor Arthur W. Peirce from Dean Academy.

In his speech, Peirce said, "Fortunate is the town whose history and tradition leads back to some memorable event or some eminent man. Lexington, Concord, Plymouth have a priceless heritage in their historic past; a heritage that not only adds luster to these names, but inspires a high degree of civic pride in their citizens. History has given them a name and place that sets them in a class apart from other municipalities..."

The celebration did not end there. The Franklin Business Association prepared a pamphlet that included tidbits on Franklin industry and history, an abundance of photographs, and the program for the bicentennial. Franklin High School students attended a stereopticon lecture on Benjamin Franklin at Dean Academy, and all students were encouraged to attend the same lecture a day later at the Morse Opera House.

President Theodore Roosevelt ordered his assistant to prepare a medallion to commemorate Franklin's birth and to present it to the town. The president's assistant followed through, and the medallion was put on display in the Ray Memorial Library along with two portraits of Benjamin Franklin. To coincide with the bicentennial event, the children's department of the Ray Memorial Library was unveiled with 1500 books initially. Interestingly, the books had been purchased with money deposited in 1848 by 16 year old Joseph G. Ray. Over the years, his initial deposit of 75 dollars had earned interest and was worth 1087.08 dollars in 1906. The annual report of the library association indicated that the original bank book, circa 1848, had been put on display in the children's room of the library as a lesson in patience and frugality. Before long, the children's department was registering almost as much foot traffic as the adult section of the library.

As the pamphlet published by the Franklin Business Association reveals, Franklinites around the turn of the century ventured out frequently on day trips across the region. This was especially true during the summer, when people from every walk of life could scrounge together a few cents to travel on one of the two major street railways in town to a nearby lake or amusement park. Trolleys operated by the Milford, Attleboro, Franklin & Woonsocket railroad competed with the Norfolk Western street railway for customers. Norfolk Western owned Hoag Lake, running excursions to it in the summer months.

Hoag Lake, located in Bellingham was later renamed Silver Lake. The lake had been used to power a mill until 1899, when the railway purchased the lake and surrounding property. An amusement park built by the street railway operated until 1922. A ride to Hoag Lake cost only five cents, and visitors could rent boats, watch vaudeville shows, swim, dance or ride on a carousel. The dance hall was located on 'Pleasure Island' in the middle of the lake. The M, A, F & W invested in a boardwalk linking the island with the shore. When the park eventually closed in the '20s, the bridge became unsafe for pedestrians and was dismantled, but the dance hall survived for years afterward. One of the most popular attractions at Hoag Lake in the early 20th century was the diving horse show featuring two white horses, King and Queen. Diving horses, such as King and Queen were trained to jump off of high wooden platforms into the waters of the lake. Today, most people would probably frown on the dangerous horse diving show at Hoag Lake, but in the early 1900s, the crowds gave little thought to the animals.

Running in the opposite direction, the trolleys would stop at Wrentham's Lake Pearl and Lake Archer. People could swim, play games, or climb aboard the small steamboat operating on Lake Pearl. At the time, almost every major pond in Massachusetts had some sort of steam launch for day excursions. In the shade of a colorful awning, fashionable passengers would enjoy the beauty of Lake Pearl as the boat ran up enough steam—and speed—to treat riders to a pleasant breeze. Day in, day out, through the summer months, the little steamer chugged from one end of the pond to the other.

Trolleys were everywhere in Franklin. Tracks ran the length of many of the main roads. A long, low brick shed that still stands today in the shadow of the Cabino bridge as a storage facility was once a shed where trolleys could go for maintenance at the end of the day (it later became home to a plow manufacturing company). Norfolk Western may have dominated the summer excursion business, but the M, A, F & W was given a monopoly on freight carrying by the Franklin government. It was given the special task of carrying newspapers, express freight, and baggage. Because of its special public role, it submitted a brief statement, in the town report.

The early 20th century resembled the late 19th century in almost every way, but change was afoot. Before many years had passed, Franklinites would be dodging automobiles on the streets, and another generation of young men who had idolized the veterans of the Cuban campaign would march off to war in Europe.

In 1908 the town chose to move away from gas lit streets, replacing its gas lamps with General Electric arc lights. Enjoying a special relation with the town government was a new Franklin based electrical company--the Union Electric Light Company--a subsidiary of a Boston company. In addition to 43 street lamps, the town was in charge of 11 fire alarm boxes under the supervision of the newly appointed Superintendent of the Fire Alarm System. However, the fire alarms had a tendency to go haywire, as the superintendent revealed in his 1905 report. "...I wish to report that the system is in good order, except about two miles of wire, which, however, is still in working condition. There has been the usual amount of trouble from cross wires and from thunder storms." In other words, the system sometimes went off during summer thunder storms, leading to some serious confusion.

Another newly minted position was that of tree warden. The tree warden was charged with planting, trimming and generally looking after the many shade trees that lined the roads. People wearing dark, heavy garments, walking along miles of scorched roadway during the summer months often succumbed to heat stroke, making shade trees an absolute necessity. Part of the tree warden's job was to spray trees to prevent brown tail moth and elm tree beetle infestation—two insect species known to decimate shade trees.

The Franklin tree warden also had to worry about gypsy moths. In 1906, he found no evidence of 'gipsy' moth infestation in the town, but the next year he was fighting a pitched battle with them. According to Robert J. Spear, author of *The Great Gypsy Moth War*, gypsy moths spread across the country from an eccentric entrepreneur's Medford garden (the man believed that he could create an especially hardy hybrid of silk and gypsy moths, making himself rich). The moths began laying eggs that produced generation after generation of voracious caterpillars, which devoured trees wherever they appeared. Problems quickly became so bad that the Alden Club and the Franklin Business Association had to donate money to the fight.

In other day-to-day news, the Franklin lock-up was becoming increasingly busy. The usual lock-up crowd of 'tramps' and drunks was supplemented with at least a few adulterers and burglars. Two individuals arrested in 1905 were simply "insane" while two others were arrested for "Sunday gaming." But none of these people were as *criminal* as one individual, arrested for selling dry goods without a license!

Adding to their list of duties, the three full time janitors, employed by Franklin schools were sworn in as truant officers, to fight truancy whenever and wherever it appeared. Barge drivers (running 'barge' wagons to schools—the horse drawn predecessor to the school bus) often had great difficulty getting students to behave. One barge driver charged with transporting almost 50 students to the North Franklin school, while managing a team of horses, had a particularly onerous task; so onerous in fact, that the School Committee recommended that North Franklin students take the street railway. "With a conductor in charge and other older passengers present, far better deportment would ensue."

Annie Ray Thayer continued in the generous vein that had seen the building of the Ray Memorial Library. On September 21, 1907, she unveiled the new Ray school, paid for with her own money.

The Ray family had been amongst the richest in Franklin since at least the 1840s, but their moderate wealth had not placed them in the same league as the great railroad tycoons and industrialists living throughout New England in the late 1800s. However, by the early 1900s, the family was taking steps to becoming Carnegies and Rockefellers in their own right. In 1909, Joseph Ray bought an entire township in northern Maine. Township Seven, Range Nine, North Waldo patent was one of the largest land purchases in New England at the time, and transformed Ray into one of largest land owners in Massachusetts, with more land to his name than some European kings.

When asked by interviewers about the secret to his success, Joseph Ray replied, "The secret of my success is hard work. I never shirk labors and never leave to others what I can do myself. My likes and dislikes? I don't know that I have any very pronounced eccentricities. I transact my business in the cold, unsympathetic rules of right and wrong."

Ray was no liar. His father, Edgar (former owner of the Milford, Franklin & Providence Railroad, and considered to be the 'electric rail king' of Rhode Island) offered his son a job as a farm hand after graduating college, that paid a dollar and a quarter, a day. Joseph took the job on the enormous Ray farm in Franklin, getting up at four a.m. each morning to milk the cows. Only after passing his father's test of humility, did Joseph Ray inherit the Ray fortune.

Even with multi-millions at his disposal, Ray remained extremely humble, dressing plainly and speaking simply. "Somehow, society doesn't interest me at all, and although I can tell you the good points of a milch cow [sic] off-hand I haven't the least idea of what society is doing at present."

What was society doing back in 1909? Although Joseph Ray was referring to high society, records from around the turn of the century give an interesting look into the interactions of people in Franklin, and the state as a whole.

At the turn of the 20th century, many racial, religious and social prejudices were deep seated. In New England, most people came from 'Yankee' backgrounds, descended from English and Scottish-American families with deep roots in the region, and typically a Protestant religious affiliation. Irish, Italian and French Canadian immigrants made up most Catholic communities. The Protestants and Catholics did not always get along well and even different Protestant sects sometimes had disputes. In fact, intermarriage between different ethnic and religious groups was uncommon. In spite of many different prejudices, Franklin was a pretty diverse place in the early 1900s.

Edward Wilder, an engineering and public health expert, included population data from the 1905 state census in his *Sanitary Survey of Franklin*. According to the census, most people in town were considered 'native,' (namely Yankee families that had lived in town since the time of the American Revolution). Other major groups included immigrants-- Irish, Italians, French Canadians, Germans, and more recent English immigrants. The census even broke down immigrants from Canada by province—including Nova Scotia, New Brunswick, Prince Edward Island, and 'English' Canada (Ontario) as separate categories!

Other immigrant groups were very small--take for example the five Belgians, three Cubans, and three Swiss, in town. Even smaller numbers of people hailed from Mexico, Austria, Denmark, and China. Created at a time when racial discrimination and classification was not uncommon, the census even had a breakdown for the six African-Americans who had come to town, escaping the poverty of the deep South.*

Before women received the right to vote, they were not included in another catalogue of local population—the poll tax list. The publicly available list showed the name and age of different voters, whether or not they had paid their tax to vote, and what their occupation was. Although not included in the list, many women *did* have jobs outside of the home at mills or shops.

Children who lived in Franklin were typically born in Franklin. Even after the Milford hospital maternity ward opened in 1918, most Franklinites were born at home. Many children did not make it past a young age—without antibiotics or vaccines even relatively mild diseases could be fatal.

Without modern disease fighting techniques, the town turned to personal hygiene to prevent diseases. The town quarantined individuals with scarlet fever and typhoid, and took preventive measures to avoid

* *Interestingly, the statistics include separate categories for 'Negroes' and 'Orientals.' In fact, even birth certificates included a line for, "Color."*

cases in a 1902 outbreak of smallpox, although tuberculosis proved harder to stop. To stop outbreaks of deadly diseases such as diphtheria, the town requested doses of 'anti-toxin,' from the state supply, and employed a health officer to fumigate houses where cases cropped up.

The town figured that it was doing everything right, but an outsider's opinion can sometimes be helpful. In 1917, Edward Wilder was asked to prepare a special report on sanitation in Franklin, after touring local farms, school, wells, ponds, and even mills.

When Wilder came to town, he started by looking into town plumbing. In 1917, some of Franklin's 1,065 houses were supplied by private wells, although most of town (especially downtown Franklin) was supplied by 30 miles of pipes with a water main leading to Unionville. In 1884, the Franklin Water Company had begun drawing water from Beaver Pond, the first attempt at a town water supply. The state got worried as years went on that the water was to dirty for drinking. The town bought up the Water Company, in 1907, and dug wells at Beaver Pond's sandy southern shore. A few years later, the town built a pumping station to pump water into the center of town.

The station was capable of pumping one and a half million gallons of water a day, from its main pump. Three other pumps, built by different companies were kept in reserve, able to pump similar amounts of water. The whole operation was powered with two boilers. Although the water was not filtered, it proved to be far cleaner than the water extracted from the pond itself, and the state approved.

Beaver Pond is linked to the Charles River by Mine Brook. In World War I, Mine Brook was still a source of power for the Norfolk Woolen Company a group that owned one of the few mills near Beaver Pond. To generate power, the company had dammed up Mine Brook, flooding a meadow, and creating a mill pond that was larger than Beaver Pond itself. Because the mill was one of the important employers in town, a small cluster of houses and barns, with accompanying cesspools and manure piles had grown up alongside it.

Mine Brook begins on the southern side of Beaver Pond, and passed behind a few farmhouses, but most of the farmers were conscientious about dumping. However, because of the dam put in place by previous mill owners, the flow of water from Beaver Pond into the Charles River was slowed, turning the pond into an almost stagnant body of water--the perfect breeding ground for microbes, an especially dangerous situation when heavy rains led to manure runoff from the farms.

In Wilder's time, only the downtown had access to town sewers. The Water and Sewer Commissioners, a group of three elected commissioners ran the town's two treatment plants at Mine Brook and

Timnah Brook. The treatment plant at Timnah Brook was close to the railroad tracks and the Golding factory (currently the white Thomason press building) in a swampy meadow far from any houses. Sewage was spread across four sandy 'beds,' where it would sink into the ground.

In 1915, the town built a larger plant on Mine Brook. The new plant was farther from the places where people lived, and stank less in the summer as a result. The plant worked much like Timnah Brook, but was even more elaborate. Dried sewage was collected and sold in town as fertilizer to raise money for the town. In the Wilder's words, "The water as it flows from the filters into Mine Brook is so clear that the Constructing Engineer confident of the efficiency of the process is reported to have drunken a glass of it." The engineer must have been *extremely* confident in his system!

Most people in town used cesspools and outhouses at their homes. The problem with cesspools, of course, was the smell. From time to time these pits needed to be cleaned, a business so disgusting that it was prohibited during the summer, and during daylight hours.

Cleaning cesspools was a foul business and a task usually accomplished with a bit of rule breaking. Many people hauled privy contents through the streets in leaky carts covered only by flimsy pieces of canvas, irking public health officials. Wilder proposed that until every house was connected to the town sewers, the evil business of cleaning cesspools, "...Might be accomplished by licensing but one party and thus forcing all business to him so that he could afford to maintain apparatus, or by the purchasing of the same by the town and the renting of it to private parties."

For his survey, Wilder made sure to visit farms in town, to see how clean they were. At the turn of the century, farms covered most of Franklin's landscape. Dairy farming was a difficult business. Big dairy processors and shippers were able to dictate prices to farmers, making big profits, at the expense of their suppliers. With demand for dairy products skyrocketing in Boston, big dairy companies began contracting with different railroads to run milk trains out into the countryside. Each day, farmers would get up in the wee hours of the morning to milk their cows, and load jugs of fresh milk aboard boxcars on the returning milk trains.

Major processors included C. Brigham Company (that later launched the famed ice cream label), H.P. Hood, Elm Farm Company and others. Hood 'owned' the North Shore and New Hampshire, while Brigham controlled central Massachusetts, including towns such as Palmer and Ware. Elm Farm bought milk from farmers in southeastern Massachusetts and Connecticut, with its trains making stops in places such as Franklin, Bellingham, Milford, Norfolk, and City Mills. Out of 39 Franklin dairy farms, Wilder was able to visit three of the largest ones.

The first stop on his tour was the Ray Farm Dairy in Unionville (present day Garelick Farms). The farm was owned by the wealthy Ray family, but Elm Farm controlled its everyday operation. The Ray's 48 soy fed cows passed Wilder's inspection with flying colors, unlike the second farm on West Central Street. There, Wilder was worried about the dairy storage tank—jugs kept cool by spring water, were exposed to the air. The last dairy on his tour received an abysmal score. Wilder almost gagged at the sight of piles of manure, the filth on barn windows, and the lack of grazing room for the cattle.

Despite his varied complaints about the third dairy on Lincoln Street, it was one of its smaller suppliers that worried him most of all. The dairy cows lived in the barn cellar. "The ceiling was low and afforded too little air space. The atmosphere was damp and heavy. An uncovered house drain ran thru [sic] one end of the room." Adding to the problem, "The well which the water for the cows was obtained was open to pollution." To top it all off, Wilder wrote, "Finally, the milker is a young man who was told he must go to the country to live because of 'lung troubles.'" To an expert like Wilder, 'lung troubles,' could mean only one thing—a tuberculosis infection. Areas with lower air pollution attracted tuberculosis victims, hoping to cure themselves. But for those unable to afford time 'in the country,' the county hospital loomed as the only option. Tuberculosis hospitals were much like prisons, quarantining their patients on a permanent basis.

In addition to the four commercial dairy farms that he visited, Wilder also called briefly at the town poor farm. "It is a three story building of wood which houses at present eight persons, five men and three women. Each of the occupants has a room of his or her own, simply but neatly furnished and lighted by one window. Heating is by hot water." Men and women lived in separate parts of the building and house was connected to town water and had flush toilets. However, the toilets were connected to a cesspool rather than the town sewer. Never idle, the inmates were productive farmers. In fact, according to Wilder, "The farm produces its own milk under better conditions than most of the other dairies in the town." For those too old, or too sick to work, the poor farm included a small infirmary that often held as many as 10 patients, receiving medical attention.

Although most milk was usually sold in the city, 18 dealers sold milk in town, after passing inspection by the Health Officer. One man served as an agent of the town, and the state Board of Health, shutting down offending businesses. Similarly a Slaughtering Inspector oversaw livestock owners and butchers.

Many farms raised sheep, beef cattle and pigs. The largest 'piggery' was on Oak Street, and supplied many animals to a small slaughterhouse in eastern Franklin. Wilder described the slaughterhouse as, "...literally an antebellum [before the Civil War] structure, having been built in the [18] '60s. It is a shed of wood about 10x15 feet, lighted by two small windows both on the same side of the building. The floor consists of loose planking. The interior is dark, none too clean, and contains a large brick furnace or oven, a bench, and the required tackle for slaughtering." A small stream ran underneath the building to drain away waste.

The Slaughtering Inspector made frequent visits to the slaughterhouse to hunt for a host of nasty diseases that sometimes affect livestock, and his eyes were the only thing that stood between Franklinites and ailments such as tape worms, hog cholera and anthrax. In theory, animals sick with tuberculosis were supposed to be disposed of in an oven, but more often the inspector made exceptions as Wilder noted. "Questioned in regard to his inspection, he replied that ordinarily he could tell by the appearance of the flesh whether or not it was fit for food. He made no examination for any specific disease other than tuberculosis. He knew the appearance of a tubercle and stated that if but one or two were found he removed them with his knife and passed the carcass [sic]."

Wilder visited three local markets that sold meat from the town slaughterhouse to see how it was handled. Most of the markets had ice cabinets where meat was kept except when being shown to a prospective customer. However, many farmers and people on the outskirts of town could not afford the time needed to get into town to purchase meat and other food. Therefore, at least one of the markets sent out a butcher with a wagon loaded up with fresh meat to supply outlying homes. "The fact that the butcher must be in and out of the cart and handling the reins, horse and money [as] well as the meat means that the latter will not be as clean as that purchased direct in the stores. On the other hand, this method of house to house peddling is necessary in the outlying districts and apparently is carried on in the cleanest manner possible." At the end of each trip, the wagon would bring any unsold meat back to store. Another house-to-house peddler sold ice cream all around town, making weekly rounds to the various neighborhoods and houses.

Before chemical refrigeration became commonplace, ice was needed to keep products such as ice cream and meat cold. When conducting his survey, Wilder visited two ponds that supplied ice for local use and for sale in Boston. Dozens of men would spend each winter cutting and storing pond ice with special tools. Franklin Ice Company owned Spring Pond on Washington Street, and passed state inspections while Green Pond on King Street (later renamed Spruce Pond) raised concerns because of the murkiness of its water, and the proximity of a piggery. Elsewhere in town, a man named Jarvis built an ice house on the shores of Beaver Pond, to harvest from the pond each winter.

Serious pollution of rivers, swamps and ponds was normal but still alarmed people like Wilder. Laws were extremely lax, and factories dumped all of their waste into nearby wetlands. Wilder noted the filth in a swamp alongside Beaver Pond. "The observer, walking out to the opposite shore to inspect the driven wells finds that the low, grass-covered viaduct over which he walks, and thru [sic] which passes the water from these wells serves to dam up a filthy, stinking scum of many colors except in one place where, borne on the surface of the combined inlet, it seeps slowly and sluggishly into the pond."

Other problems included impromptu dumps in virtually every neighborhood. Wilder visited three, the first on Alpine Place next to a small immigrant neighborhood. "Hay, old bedding, paper, tin cans, sweepings from the smithy and other rubbish were on the dump. There was practically no odor, but the dump is an eye-sore as well as being unsanitary and should be abolished," he wrote. The dump was so full, that trash was spilling into neighboring vegetable gardens.

The second dump that Wilder visited, he described as, "A dump which is more of a menace is the one which has already been mentioned in connection with the water supply and which is located on Beaver Street." The dump was located in between Mine Brook and Beaver Pond, near the present soccer field. "This comes, perhaps, nearer to being a public dump than any of the others as dumping was allowed here by the authorities until recently, when, at the [insistence] of the Health Agent, a sign prohibiting dumping was erected by order of the selectmen. The warning is not, however, heeded nor the statute enforced as is showing by the following incident." After visiting the dump on one day to photographs of the heap of hay, straw, papers and old tin cans, Wilder returned a few days later to find rotting fruit heaped added to the pile.

Wilder offered his own proposal for an official town dump. "If Franklin is to have a public dump it should be located at a point distant from dwellings and water supply. All dumping should be then limited to that one site." He suggested that some household waste, such as ashes ought to be better used fertilizing fields and paving roads than filling up dumps.

The final stops on Wilder's tour were a few of Franklin's schools. By 1917, the schools were not as rustic as they had been in 1870s and '80s, but some were still quite primitive. The rural district schools—such as Unionville and South Franklin—still had 'privies,' although most schools had installed flush toilets and other modern conveniences such as showers. The young superintendent doubled as high school principal, and struck Wilder as, "intensely interested in his job." The school system left him with a good impression.

Franklin schools were down to 10, from 18 in the 1880s. Some older schools such as City Mills had been shuttered although only three of the schools were new brick buildings. Each day horse drawn barges, carried students to school, and then took them home in the afternoons. High School classes began at eight-thirty in the morning and continued until noon. At noon, students could either walk to their houses for lunch, or eat their meals at the High School. An hour later, at one o'clock, classes resumed until three o'clock in the afternoon.

Wilder realized that climate control in school buildings was a necessity, but achieving that goal in 1917 was a difficult job. Janitors (then tasked with heating buildings during the cold months) were ordered to keep the schools between 65 and 68 degrees. Sometimes, however, teachers forced the janitor to ratchet the heat up to 70 degrees, but since none of the schools had thermostats it was all guesswork. The newer schools had modern heating systems, but the old district schools still relied on stoves to keep students warm.

With the exception of the district schools, all of Franklin's schools had electric lights in 1917. However, natural light was still the order of the day, and schools were designed with sunlight in mind. According to Wilder, the aim was to arrange desks and chairs so that sunlight fell on the chalkboard but not in a student's eyes.

Edward Wilder's highly detailed report might not make the best pleasure reading, but the inspections and observations he made in the summer of 1917, provides a unique and lasting record of Franklin's most mundane aspects. Thanks to the work of people such as Wilder, Franklin was able to continue growing as a town, slowly fixing its waste, pollution, and public health problems over the course of years.

All images courtesy of the Franklin Historical Commission, originally produced by Edward Wilder, and donated to the town in 1966 by his wife.

The settling ponds of the Mine Brook treatment plant in Unionville, processed Franklin's waste well in the 1970s, taking the load off of the smaller Timnah Brook plant.

The smelly settling ponds at the Timnah Brook plant, Franklin's earliest sewage plant, sometimes bothered downtown residents during the summer. This image was taken looking to north, toward the Golding Mfg. Co. building, today known as Thomason Press.

Before a central dump was created, town trash accumulated in impromptu dumps found in almost every neighborhood. In this picture, trash is overflowing into an adjacent war garden, on Alpine Street.

To supply local customers, farmers sent their sheep, cattle, and hogs to this small slaughterhouse in eastern Franklin.

A typical dairy barn may have held a few dozen cows. With over 39 dairies in 1917, Franklin had plenty of milk to export.

To expand the food supply during the shortages imposed by World War I, many people planted war gardens (center).

Mine Brook pond, created by a small dam on Mine Brook to power neighboring mills, existed until the 1950s, when the dam burst during a hurricane. The pond was larger than neighboring Beaver Pond.

Chapter 12:

1918 - The Darkest Year

..."The local board of health wishes to strongly impress upon the people of Franklin that they should visit as little as possible, at this time, and under no circumstances to visit a home where there are patients ill with influenza."...

The years leading up to World War I were some of the best since the 1880s for Franklin. A few new companies and groups started—for example, the Loyal Order of Moose lodge, and the Clark, Cutler, McDermott company on Fisher Street manufacturing non-woven horse blankets.

From 1912 through 1917, the *Franklin Sentinel* reported an endless cycle of speeches, outings, conferences and suppers held by the Odd Fellows, the Red Men, and various church communities. Everybody had ideas, and frequent formal dinners gave people a chance to hear some pretty unusual ones--the brother of the superintendent of schools presented a paper on eugenics while another man planned to institute a curfew for young people by ringing the town fire bell at nine p.m. each night. Even with so many events to keep up with the *Sentinel* often had so little to print, that the editors included lists of unclaimed letters at the post office, in need of pickup.

The Grand Army of the Republic added the Newell Relic and Curio Hall to their meetinghouse* with funds from the generous Frederick Newell (the same man who paid for the Civil War monument on the common). Newell was apparently fascinated by military history, and after making himself a fortune had set about collecting memorabilia from the Civil War and American Revolution. After the state bought his mansion in Attleboro to build a courthouse, he needed a new home for his collection, and paid for the GAR 'Curio Hall,' in Franklin. In its day, the Curio Hall may have been one of the biggest war museums in the country, but the fate of Newell's donation is unknown.

Judging by the suggestions of the State Board of Agriculture, farming must have been going well. In their 1911 special report on farming resources, they wrote that, "Every town [in southeastern Massachusetts, including Franklin, Braintree, and Weymouth] has a

* The GAR hall was already a large meetinghouse, used by the GAR, the Women's Relief Corps, Spanish War Veterans, and Sons and Daughters of Veterans. The building was still standing and in use until at least the 1930s.

railroad station and most of them two or three. These serve an immense suburban population...[that] does business in Boston...Poultry, vegetables, and small fruits can be raised for profit and pleasure by the commuter, and the satisfaction of owning a piece of old Mother Earth enjoyed." The report was suggesting that city dwellers take advantage of low property prices in town, to set up small farms that would allow them to reach their jobs in Boston by rail, while supplying their own food. Now that's a very different idea of the suburban dream!

The town hall was renovated in 1916, the Episcopalians built a new church, Sheldonville (West Wrentham) received electric power for the first time, and a group of Christian Scientists began meeting in the old Odd Fellows hall. The Knights of Columbus built a lodge, and added to Franklin's lively social life. With busy social lives and business days, most people could afford to ignore the ongoing war in Europe until April, 1917.

When the US went to war with Germany, the *Sentinel* hardly mentioned it. Instead, the groundbreaking news that day was a report on the notorious typewriter thieves at the high school, on the run from Chief Knowlton (the typewriters were discovered in the woods off of Wachusett Street). It seems surprising that the *Sentinel* would ignore such a pivotal event. After all, dozens of Franklin men enlisted, and eight of them never returned home.

Edward Wilder's report gives some idea of the wartime commitment of Franklin families—tilling abandoned lots into garden plots. But his report does not give a very clear picture of the extreme hardship that many people faced during the war.

As rationing took effect, common household items became scarce. At first, the shortages were only problematic but by the frigid winter of 1917 and 1918, the scarcity of many goods was making everyday life extremely difficult in Franklin. Some minor celebration took place but plummeting temperatures and rationing put a damper on New Year's festivities for 1918. The *Sentinel* reported one of the coldest weeks in living memory. "With none too much coal to keep off the chill winds, this [town], and in fact all New England, has been held since Friday night in the grasp of the coldest snap of the present winter, the mercury being down from 15 to 24 degrees below zero some of the nights."

In drafty New England houses, Arctic temperatures such as these would make keeping warm a struggle even in normal circumstances. But the winter of 1918 was not a typical winter. Extreme shortages of food and fuel made homes colder than ever, and left many underfed. Coal particularly was snatched up by the government to keep the wheels of industry turning and to keep American troops and their allies in

Europe warm during the long winter. Warmth in France and England came at the expense of towns like Franklin.

Franklinites were encouraged to join 'Cut-a Cord-Clubs,' heading out into woods in the dead of winter to cut fuel to heat their houses. "Make a winter outing of this chopping bee, with the women and children along to prepare the hot luncheon over the campfire..." read an enthusiastic tidbit in *Sentinel*. Although the idea of 'hot luncheon' in the woods eaten with friends and family sounds pleasant, the winter of 1918 was one of the few times in 20th century Franklin when many Franklinites had to fight to survive.

The Trowbridge piano factory was nearly destroyed by fire on January 18, when barrels of cotton at a neighboring mill caught fire near midnight. Luckily the fire was extinguished before the factory could be totally ruined. Many businesses were barely scraping by. The shoddy mill changed hands, the Medway and Dedham railroad company ended service to Franklin, even the Milford, Attleboro and Woonsocket street railroad serving Franklin, Bellingham and Wrentham raised its rates. The Ray Memorial Library was forced to cut its hour to only two days a week during the winter of 1918 due to the coal shortage and local businesses were forbidden to burn any fuel for heating. The *Sentinel* was forced to cut its page count from eight to four because of the national paper shortage.

A huge effort was underway to win the war and by order of the government all of Franklin's factories closed down and sent their employees home for more than a week at the end of January. For the rest of the week, rail lines in Franklin were taken over by War Department coal trains carrying thousands of tons of coal to harbors and ports where it could be shipped to Europe. One of the only exceptions to this rule may have been the enormous Caryville mill that ran day and night, churning out tens of thousands of silk cartridge bags. Extreme cold claimed a number of lives, including May Alden, founder of the Alden Club, who fell ill and died. As coal became increasingly scarce, so did food. Franklinites virtually abandoned butter and lard in their cooking and eating and skipped eating red meat on two days each week. Mondays and Wednesdays were considered 'wheatless' days.

Franklin women were told to be vigilantly conservative with food scraps. They were told not to feed scraps to hogs, but to turn them over to be processed into glycerin for munitions. Even peach pits were saved to use in gas masks. To fill the gap in food supplies people signed up to take classes on poultry care at the Norfolk County agricultural school. Franklinites banded together, forming a community kitchen to can and jar fruits and vegetables. Even high school students, when spring and summer finally rolled around, pitched in to raise crops. Dean contributed to the war effort, as well, slashing their athletic programs, and offering military training instead.

During the war, reformers circulated through town trying to convince people to give up another part of daily life, in this case, alcohol, as the temperance movement was gearing up for nationwide prohibition.

Residents of Franklin experienced all of the hardships of the home front but the war was not a picnic for Franklin soldiers. Woodrow Wilson had enacted a draft and small groups of Franklin men were called up every few weeks during 1918. In a show of public spiritedness, one group of conscripts was given wristwatches by the town public safety committee. Most soldiers were sent to Fort Devens in Ayer, Massachusetts for training.

Each day, the *Sentinel* printed poems and songs that ranged from patriotic to silly. Supposedly, Franklin soldiers at Fort Devens were familiar with a poem known as the *New Deven's Dirge*:

Sherman said that war was hell,

'Twas fifty years ago.

But Sherman never was at Ayer,

So Sherman did not know.

Hell is hot, but Ayer is not,

It's twenty-eight below;

That's why we're going over there.

Franklin conscripts and volunteers training at Fort Devens had limited opportunities to see friends and family face to face. To cheer up the young soldiers from Franklin, local families bought 'Smileage' books that contained tickets to vaudeville variety shows held frequently in Ayer. Once in a while, though, the soldiers got away from Fort Devens for short visits to Franklin. In the 1918 governor's election, the hundreds of voters who turned up at the polls in Franklin included plenty of local men stationed in Ayer.

Most Franklinites involved in the war were men but a handful of women served in France as nurses. Mabel Johnson, a young Red Cross nurse who had recently arrived in Paris, wrote home to her parents who lived on School Street. Her letter was printed in the *Sentinel*. Mabel had been astounded by the beauty of Paris, even in wartime, and was especially impressed by her tour of the Seine River with her friends. "I told the girls tonight at dinner that I was beginning to think it was my birthday... I hope Mr. Censor does not cut too much of this letter out.

There are a great many Americans here, I mean of course, in uniform. I am learning French slowly, but manage to get about quite well."

Other soldiers serving in France were not as quick to pick up French. Lt. Robert H. Wehknet a 1909 graduate of Dean Academy had his letter published in the *Sentinel*. "I still know only the 25 or 30 short words I knew shortly after I landed....The staff eats at an officers' mess, not in a private family, which would be most desirable. It is surprising how easily one can make himself understood even when restricted to but the fewest words. A short time ago I had occasion to buy an elbow for a stove pipe. The only French words I knew which had any relation to this were 'feu' and 'fumee'—I don't vouch for the spelling. I went into a hardware shop, spoke the proper greeting: 'bon jour, madame!' and then without more words looked about until I saw a stove." After gesticulating and using his tiny vocabulary, the Lieutenant finally purchased the stove pipe elbow.

For German-Americans living in Franklin, life could be extremely hard. Even friends and neighbors became suspicious, suspecting them of enemy sympathies. The superintendent went so far as to investigate the school German program for spreading German propaganda. German teachers objected but kept quiet, fearing that they would lose their jobs. Luckily, the German textbook passed the superintendent's inspection, although many other towns had thrown away all of their copies.

In the early autumn of 1918, the Spanish influenza pandemic that had begun earlier in the year, spread to America. Transported in the lungs of returning soldiers, the national epidemic was kindled in Massachusetts—the first cases were reported in two sailors at Boston's Commonwealth Pier -- and spread like wild fire across the country. Franklin felt the impact of this deadly strain of influenza. Within a week, 100 new cases had been reported, and throughout the fall of 1918, nearly a quarter of the US population would be taken ill with the new strain of influenza.

There was no advance warning; locals contracted the disease and died soon after, spreading it to friends, family members and neighbors. Two Dean students died, and the illness spread quickly across town.

A well-known local restaurant owner died of the disease along with a teacher at the Unionville school. Franklinites were terrified. Some people even believed that raking up and burning leaves could spread the virus. Although they attempted to reason with people, the members of the local Board of Health were probably as bewildered as everyone else. Recommendations from the Board of Health were published in the *Sentinel*. "The local board of health wishes to strongly impress upon the people of Franklin that they should visit as little as possible, at this time, and under no circumstances to visit a home where there are patients ill with influenza."

Town doctors were overwhelmed with cases and to save time traveling between houses a temporary hospital was set up in the town hall (the present day Franklin Historical Museum), run by the District Nurse. The hospital had as many as 30 beds, operating for a few weeks until the epidemic burnt itself out. Then the town hall was fumigated and the hospital cleared away. Meanwhile, the town's social life had ground to a halt. Church services and Sunday school were cancelled, restaurants and schools closed. Even the popular dance hall at Wrentham's Lake Pearl was closed.

By October 25, the epidemic had begun to resolve itself and the Board of Health agreed to reopen churches within a week, but only allowed healthy individuals over the age of 15 to attend services. In addition, ice cream vendors and soda fountains began operating again, but on condition that they use disposable paper plates and cups. Schools stayed closed.

The *Sentinel* typically avoided printing news about war casualties—considering such stories to be defeatist. In a few cases, the newspaper included accounts of Dean students for their acts of heroism. Nonetheless, casualties were hard to ignore, especially when Edward Grant was killed in France by an exploding shell.

Grant was a Franklin hero. Born in 1883, he moved from the minor to the major leagues and became a well-known baseball player for the Phillies, Reds, and Giants. In addition to being an excellent player, Grant was extremely intelligent. After retiring from professional ball in 1915, he used his Harvard degree to become an attorney, and when war broke out, he enlisted as an officer.

The day after the armistice went into effect the town held an impromptu celebration. Bonfires were lit all over the Dean campus, and all the fraternal organizations paraded through the downtown. Coal rationing was lifted, but Herbert Hoover, the head of the food administration (and future president), encouraged everyone to maintain 'victory gardens' to fight communism.

During the war, Woodrow Wilson had enacted laws that prevented anyone from disagreeing openly with the war. Wilson attempted to limit the ability of workers to strike. After the war, the US government began going after suspected communists, fearful that some leftists would try to overthrow the government. In Massachusetts, Italian anarchist Luigi Galleani enjoyed widespread support amongst mill workers. The crimes that he masterminded, and the ideas he espoused made him one of the most wanted men in America, and his capture in Wrentham was sensational news.

On March 4, 1919, a few of Galleani's sympathizers tried to bomb the Hayward mill on Union Street. According to the *Sentinel*, "Dwellers in Franklin and residents outside as far as Milford, Dedham, Norton and elsewhere heard about 8.45, Friday evening, a muffled report, which to different ears sounded differently. Residents on McCarthy and Sugar Beet streets asserted that they saw the smoke of an explosion back of Ray's hill, and investigation by Chief Knowlton [of the Franklin Police Department] and Fire Chief Metcalf developed the fact that there had been an explosion of some kind in the swamp below the hill, though darkness and uneven ground made it seem advisable to wait till morning before making a thorough investigation. Capt. Appleton of the State Guard was communicated with, a cordon of guards was thrown about the entire section, the State Police were notified and morning awaited."

"An early search revealed the fact that there had been victims of the explosion, and further investigation proved that the men who lost their lives were apparently bent upon destroying the mill of the American Woolen Company, only a few hundred yards distant. Apparently they had left their homes in the darkness, gone down the steep hill in the rear, and as near as can be learned one of the party was taking a quantity of dynamite from a pig pen at the foot of the hill when it exploded, killing four men, whose dismembered bodies were scattered over a large area through the swamp, upon buildings, etc., as well as shattering all of the windows and the sashes in the houses nearby."

Identifying what was left of the four bombers was a difficult business. Rain poured down, "...In sheets," for most of the day and the best that State officials and a professional medical examiner could do to identify the remains was to inquire about any missing Italian factory workers. In fact, the only indication as to the number of men involved were eight feet scattered around by the blast. By the end of the day, members of the State Guard and the general public were allowed to roam the site of the premature explosion.

Eventually the four men were identified as James Tarzin, Eustachio DeChellis, Silvario DeChellis and Dominic Palumbo. It seems that Tarzin was the one carrying the dynamite, because he had the fewest remains out of the four. The discovery of his draft card, finally confirmed his identity. Apparently, Tarzin was known as a member of the International Workers of the World, a group of radical pro-labor advocates known as 'Wobblies.'

Edward Wilder's survey offers background on Franklin mill conditions during World War I. After getting permission from the manager of the company and from the local Board of Health, Wilder toured the H.T. Hayward Company on Union Street, a factory that made woolen products (and the target of the anarchist attack). He found that employees worked 56 hours a week if they were men (54 if they were women). On average, employees worked 10 hours a day, and made up whatever time was left on Saturdays. The 175 employees worked in a well-lit and well ventilated factory, at least according to Wilder. Always pleased by modern sanitation, Wilder delighted in the water fountains on each floor and the flush toilets in the basement. He noted one concern, writing that, "No information was obtainable as to the machinery so that it was not possible to ascertain how carefully the employees were protected. There did not appear to be any very evident danger to life or limb, however. In the dye room no precautions were taken against chemical poisoning."

The Hayward mill may have been an exception, but generally speaking, Franklin mills were probably much better places to work than sweat shops in crowded cities such as Boston and New York. If nothing else, workers enjoyed 'tenements.' As Wilder points out the one and a half story homes--11 owned by the Hayward company--were not true tenements. The largest had seven rooms while the rest had between five and six rooms, plus storage space in the eaves. Inhabitants of the 'tenements' enjoyed running water and electricity, but no town sewage. The yards surrounding the houses were not sprawling estates to be sure, but Wilder wrote that the, "...Kitchen gardens are flourishing."

"The houses were very neat in appearance, were in good repair, and seemed to [be] most comfortable. The rent for the six room tenement was $1.86 per week. Little can be said in criticism of these dwellings. The one necessary feature which they lack is modern toilet facilities...Where houses are as near together as in this case it requires considerable care to prevent a privy from becoming a nuisance. As it was, a walk thru the back yards disclosed a noticeable odor." Aside from privy vapors and the 1.86 dollars per week, returned to the pockets of the Hayward company bosses, workers seemingly would have little to complain about. It is possible that the four anarchists worked for a company that did maintain good conditions for its workers, or maybe they sought to strike a blow at the 'Establishment,' in a town separated from the big, vigilant police forces of the cities by many miles. Hypothetically, a well-placed bomb might have done significant damage to the mill, but the only indication of the bomb's power was the loud blast and swift, spectacular results on the four anarchists.

Three days after the blast it was revealed in the *Sentinel* that Chief Knowlton had known all along about the anarchist leanings of the four men and had tailed them on various occasions. He had watched the comings and goings of other suspicious characters and anarchists associated with the Franklin bombers and even voiced concern to the selectmen.

So much had happened in only a few years—including a war, a pandemic, a terrorist attack, and (at the end of 1919) the start of prohibition. Of all hardships that Frankinites faced, the switch from beer to soda was probably the hardest!

Chapter 13:

The 1920s

In truth, Franklin...could still claim to be a "dear" old fashioned town.

After all the trouble caused by World War I, the 1920s were a brighter time. Although a handful of cars had puttered along Franklin roads before the war, cars became commonplace after the armistice. In fact, an automotive dealership opened in Franklin. Ironically, the dealership on Summer Street sold Franklin Touring Cars (manufactured in Syracuse, not Franklin). An advertisement for Franklin automobiles took up much of the *Sentinel's* front page. "The reason Franklin owners don't put money into shock absorbers, thermometers, radiator blankets, etc., is because their cars give satisfaction without them." In fact, Franklin cars were much more reliable than most cars of their day. Doctors and other professionals favored them because of their air cooled engines which kept Franklins running even in cold weather.

Members of the Country Club could afford to purchase new cars, as well as paying membership dues to use the club' new golf course. However, the Country Club that had existed since the turn of the century needed to be expanded. The Club rented land from Odella Nye, the daughter of the Club's original benefactress, Amanda Waite. With the Country Club's lease fast expiring, Nye was getting ready to sell the land. In March, 1921, a special meeting of the club was held to decide on a course of action. Some of those who turned up for the meeting were not even members of the Franklin Country Club, but instead were members of the Milford Country Club. The Milford crowd wanted the Franklin members to join them, but instead the club chose to speak with Nye about purchasing her land. Within a week, the club members met Nye and convinced her to sell.

To purchase and manage the land, the Franklin Country Club became a stock company, and certificates were sold to anyone who was interested in joining. The largest stock holders became the board of governors for the Franklin Country Club and together paid for a new clubhouse

The club reopened for business on Memorial Day with golf tournaments in the morning and live dance music in the evening. Its rapid growth was attracting interest from the surrounding towns and money continued to pour in, providing the needed finances for more construction. The money from new members covered not only the new clubhouse but also the salaries of a groundskeeper and an assistant groundskeeper to keep the property in tip-top condition.

Franklin's growing Catholic population suffered a serious setback in May, 1923 when the existing church burnt to the ground. Ground was broken for the current church in September, and the building was completed by 1924. The Catholic community had growing numbers of Italian-Americans who brought a lodge of the Sons of Italy to town, to compete with the Irish-American organization; the Ancient Order of Hibernians.

In 1922, the wealthy Thayer family funded the construction of a brick fire station and fire tower on West Central Street. The J.G. Ray fire station allowed the town to concentrate its fire engines in one place, rather than spreading them out among many, different fire sheds across town. The gift to the town helped to save the government money to spend on a new high school.

Horace Mann High School (which had opened in 1898), at the corner of Emmons and West Central Street, was retired in 1925, and students moved to a new building on the corner of West Central and Union Street. The old high school faced problems with crowding. Its original 57 students had swelled to 244; science labs were located on the poorly ventilated third floor, and were standing room only, and 20 people were forced to crowd into a typewriter room built for half that number. The old high school was ultimately refurbished and turned into the current recreation department building.

Before the devastating stock market crash in 1929, the town celebrated its 1928 sesquicentennial (150th anniversary). Planning committee member Grace Buchanan and Professor Arthur Peirce rehashed Mortimer Blake's 1878 history with some new photographs and additions, including a program for the sesquicentennial, for publication after the event. Stanley Chilson, a highly involved citizen, photographer, and full-time gardener, contributed many of the photographs for the town history.*

The sesquicentennial celebration lasted three days, and included bands, block dancing, a parade, and a historical pageant. At two p.m. after the parade a concert on the common, put on by the Worcester Brass Band, was followed with speeches by famous men from Franklin and around the state. Arthur Peirce contributed his two cents worth, but he may have been overshadowed by more illustrious company. The

From the 1920s to the 1960s, Chilson documented, in still and moving pictures, many aspects of Franklin life—from fires, to summer baseball games—leaving an excellent record of 20th century Franklin life.

Lieutenant Governor spoke along with James Michael Curley, Boston's mayor and a future Massachusetts governor. At eight o'clock p.m. a historical pageant was performed at Grant Field (Dean Academy), and at ten o'clock, a fireworks display was put on.

The historical pageant was an impressive piece of choreography involving dozens of local men, women and children. The pageant was broken into 'episodes' beginning with the 'wilderness.' People were cast as flowers, lakes and trees. Episode II covered the arrival of colonists from Dedham, while Episode III covered the rout of the warriors at Indian Rock, and so on. Episode XI covered the "Gay Nineties" with a recreated husking bee, while Episode XV focused on Franklin's World War I contribution.

A man named Reignold K. Marvin, D.D. prepared the *Song of our Franklin* to the tune of "America the Beautiful."

With willing feet and eager eyes,

Today we gladly turn,

Where old familiar places rise,

And kindled memories burn.

O Franklin Town, O Franklin Town,

Our praise to thee we bring,

An honest pride in honest worth,

What better can we sing?

For here, secure from care and noise

Sits in her home spun gown,

To greet her grown-up girls and boys,

The dear old fashioned town.

O Franklin Town, O Franklin Town,

The place that gave us birth,

May future years thy glory spread

To all the spacious earth!

In truth, Franklin, even after decades of immigration, could still claim to be a "dear old fashioned town." The 1928 population (estimated based upon the 1925 census) was only 7,055. Diminutive, perhaps, but the population had increased threefold in the space of only fifty years. In 1878, the town could claim only 2,893 inhabitants. Franklin was also the largest town in western Norfolk County—smaller than Milford, Attleboro, or Woonsocket, but more significant than its close neighbors.

In 1929, the town added two monuments. The Horace Mann monument, located on roughly the same spot as the old Mann farm, was unveiled on Saturday, May 4, 1929, an event met with a small celebration. The Franklin High School band played Sousa's *Washington Post*, and school children in fifth and sixth grade sang. Professor Peirce contributed his comments, but the crowd (especially Catholics come to watch the unveiling) must have been particularly interested to hear Senator David I. Walsh give his "Tribute to the Nation" address. After all, Walsh was the first Roman Catholic governor of Massachusetts. The ceremony, attended by Mann descendants, was concluded with the placing of a floral wreath on the monument by the last surviving charter member of the Franklin Grange, and the singing of the 'Star Spangled Banner."

A different and more somber event was held on November 11, 1929, coming on the heels of the stock market crash. Before it became known as Veterans' Day, November 11 was referred to as Armistice Day--the day on which World War I came to an end. The Committee on the World War Memorial planned to dedicate the new monument on Armistice Day. Planning had begun earlier in the year, in coordination with the American Legion. It was decided that the monument would be built on the north end of the common. It would have a circular base, made from granite. A bronze soldier with his head bowed would be the centerpiece. The monument was planned to be a less costly copy of a monument in Connecticut.

As the 1920s came to an end on a sour note, Franklin – like most of the nation -- faced an uncertain road ahead.

These images of Franklin around the turn of the 20th century portray an interesting picture of the downtown; looking north along Main Street (top) and southeast along East Central Street, the town center is crowded with horse drawn carts and trolleys. Note the trolley track in the center of the road, and the landmark water fountain for horses, still in the same location today (top).

The Civil War monument on the common was donated by Frederick A. Newell, a local benefactor whose collection of military artifacts was donated to the Grand Army of the Republic as a 'Curio Hall.' (Franklin Historical Commission)

Donated in 1904 by the daughters of wealthy local entrepreneur, Joseph G. Ray, the current library building was managed by a private organization for decades.

Typical of worker's housing around the turn of the century, this Hayward 'tenement' was leased to employees and their families.

Franklin's 150th anniversary in 1928 was a major cause for celebration, Clark Square is decked out with a banner for the occasion.

This man appears to have the right idea, selling balloons for the sesquicentennial.

Chapter 14:

The Great Depression

...The Civilian Conservation Corps, a military-styled civil works service, set up a camp on the top of Forge Hill...

The tough economy of the 1930s forced Franklinites to live frugal and often very difficult lives, but hardship helped to strengthen the community. As everyone celebrated the start of the new year, in 1930, they hoped for better times ahead; 1929 had ended with huge problems for the nation. In the near term, people could rely on the *Sentinel* for local news, and kindling—the newspaper cost only a dollar every six months, because it was largely subsidized by local businesses. Local companies, hoping to draw in wary customers printed large ads. Harris' Garage & Battery Service advertised new Pontiacs, while the Union Light company offered a special sale on a warehouse full of Frigidaire refrigerators. Hoping to get their businesses through rough times, many business owners joined the Rotary Club, and launched a campaign to attract new companies.

The Nowland Aircraft Corporation, formed by a Franklin man, designed and built a two-seater plane and unveiled it for investors. Nowland's design interested local investors enough that they planned to build an aircraft plant in Franklin, although plans fell through.

Simon & Son Furnishers tried a different tactic to keep customers coming. In 1930, they footed the bill for the airship *Neponset* to come to Franklin. A large ground crew arrived, and set up a mooring mast for the airship, which took Franklinites on half hour flights over town.

Other businesses tried joining larger chains, to survive. For example, George Peck, Franklin's most successful grocer merged his store with the International Grocers' Alliance.

For some the Great Depression, seemed to be more of a novelty than a hardship; take for example the Ancient Order of Hibernians, who adapted to the times by offering edible prizes (in this case, a turkey) to the winner of their beauty contest. Then there was a 23 year old, female hitchhiker from New Jersey who arrived penniless in Franklin. After stopping at a farmhouse, and asking to stay in the barn, she was turned over to the police by the farmer. Because "vagrancy" was considered a crime, she spent the night in jail—fulfilling, she claimed, one of her lifelong goals. Judge James at the District Court was more sympathetic than the farmer, and let her go the next morning; the officers at the lock-up gave her a good meal to speed her to Cape Cod.

To help get Franklin back on its feet, local citizens formed the Franklin Employment Plan, and arranged a pledge drive to raise 50,000 dollars. The pledge drive was accompanied by a larger than life thermometer in Clark Square (where West Central St. and Main St. cross the railroad tracks). With each pledge the 'mercury' shot up a bit higher

An illegal cottage industry of the 1920s, held over into the early '30s, helped many families to get by. Because the state of Rhode Island did not approve of national prohibition, the state simply ignored federal laws and continued to sell alcohol. Many locals turned to 'bootlegging,' using cars, trucks and the cover of night to smuggle alcohol into Massachusetts. Others distilled their own, in abandoned barns, and out in the woods. Penalties could be steep for captured bootleggers, and although the business was widespread, it was extremely risky. Even today, almost 80 years after the end of prohibition, the children of bootleggers continue to guard the secrets of old family enterprises, and hint of it only in whispered tones.

But police were not interested in illegal distilleries when they came to town in force, at the end of 1930. As reporters poured into town from all across the country, the manhunt for Oliver Garrett continued. Although he was only a Boston patrolman, Garrett wielded as much power as the mayor, when he finally went on the run. He had everything a man could want. Between 1923 and 1929, he amassed more than a quarter million dollars, even though he officially earned only 40 dollars a week. By the end of the 1920s he owned race horses, a dairy farm (a front for an illegal liquor supply business), and numerous houses, and was spending other lavish sums on fine dining and entertainment at Boston's most glamorous hotels. He had begun his career as a straight laced, Protestant telegraphist in Maine, but had risen to an extremely powerful position as the head of the Boston police vice and liquor squad, within only four years of becoming an officer. As head of the liquor squad, Garrett was able to leverage the power and money of gangsters and bureaucrats to his own advantage. One of his greatest victories was winning the protection of the police commissioner.

Others in the police force may have been as corrupt as Garrett, because his blatantly illegal activities were long ignored. However, by 1930, the police were beginning to get wise to Garrett, and the future no longer looked so rosy for him. Claiming a fractured skull, he was examined by doctors, and insisted that the Boston police provide him with a disability pension. For Garrett, it seemed like a smart move. He could claim that his alleged head injury caused him to be irresponsible, if anyone ever dragged him into court. Garrett's pension did not work out as planned. Big city newspapers in Boston cracked his racket wide open in a series of scathing, investigative articles. Soon the Attorney General and his men were looking into Garrett's activities.

In June, he disappeared. Police were mystified, and could offer little to newspapermen clamoring for information on the fugitive. By late autumn, the newspapers had turned their attention to Franklin, where it appeared that he had been hiding out for five weeks in a rented cottage on Lincoln Street. The report of his presence came from two local men, reporting separately. One allegedly sold a pair of gloves to the wanted man, while the other spotted him, as he delivered groceries to a cottage on Lincoln Street.

The police swept in to town to investigate. The cottage was searched multiple times by the Franklin police, the Boston police, the state police, and detectives working for the District Attorney's office. Each of searches proved fruitless--the police could not figure out where Garrett was hiding, if indeed, he was still in the house. As soon as the newspapers got wind of the mysterious cottage, they lionized Garrett for his skillful evasion of the police, and insisted that he was hiding in a crawlspace under the eaves of the house.

The police did discover a secret compartment under the eaves. One officer slipped through the trapdoor into the tight compartment to ascertain whether Garrett could have fit inside. The officer fit into the compartment, but came out covered from head to toe in dust. The dust lay an inch thick in the compartment, and had not been disturbed in years.

On December 4, the police launched what could only be termed a dragnet. Eighteen state troopers, astride motorcycles, blocked all of the highways and main roads leading into and out of Franklin. Hundreds of people from out of town streamed in to see the cottage where Garrett, the great racketeer, had hid out. Chief Knowlton of the Franklin police was kept tied to his desk, answering a telephone that continued to ring. Newspaper reporters were eager for new details and developments. Some cameramen were so eager for pictures that they crossed onto land owned by the owner of the cottage. The landlord drove them off.

The police had offered to let Garrett off on bail, if he voluntarily surrendered to the police. This he finally did, walking nonchalantly into Boston's Charles Street jail just after noon. He had had quite a series of adventures since June, 1930. He hid out in Mexico and Texas before coming back to Franklin, and had nearly been caught on one occasion in North Attleboro. Rather than hiding beneath the eaves of his Lincoln Street cottage, Garett had hid in a tiny room behind a false wall that had been entirely missed by the police officers and detectives, and he had already left town by the time the police began casing Franklin.

Garrett was tried, and pleaded guilty. He was sentenced to two years in prison, a light sentence for his gross corruption.

Up until 1931, Franklin was home to the district courthouse for western Norfolk County. That year, Wrentham pushed hard to move the court house to their town (where it is located today). The state committee called to look into the proposal held a meeting in Franklin, and faced stern opposition from local residents. According to the *Sentinel*, "As soon as those in favor of the transfer had finished speaking, the chairman of the Judiciary committee asked if there was any opposition to it. 'Yes,' said Selectman Cook [of Franklin], rising to his feet, 'a whole room full of it.'"

Not everything was quite so dire. The *Sentinel* reported the capture of a notorious monkey who had been up to all sorts of mischief. A few days earlier, the monkey escaped from its handler at Attleboro's Capron Park. Soon after, a homeowner in Plainville was shocked to find that a monkey had scared her chickens off of their eggs, and was rolling the eggs around the chicken yard. The monkey was driven off, but staged a similar performance in Wrentham, dropping out of a tree to snatch chicken feed, even as the chickens' owner was in the process of feeding the birds. When the monkey stopped on a doorstep in West Wrentham, a boy tried to catch it by dangling a doughnut on a stick in front of it. The monkey outwitted the boy, grabbing and making off with the doughnut.

The monkey was next spotted by swimmers at Uncas Pond, who saw it swinging between tree branches around the pond. Although the swimmers lost sight of the monkey in the trees around the pond, it was spotted again. A crowd of Franklinites followed the monkey all the way across town, until it disappeared near the Thomason Press building. It reappeared in Medway, racing across roofs. Finally, after a few days of nonstop excitement, the monkey stopped to rest beneath a tree. Two Medway boys crept up and captured it, displaying it proudly for all to see, until its owner came to reclaim it.

In another weird incident, residents of Brook Street were stunned to see an 18 foot long, eight inch thick snake slithering through the neighborhood. The chief of police went to go talk to the circus that had just passed through town, and told Brook Street residents to stay clear of the snake. A few neighbors ignored the chief's advice and formed a posse, trying unsuccessfully to catch the escaped animal.

Novelties such as escaped monkeys and snakes helped to fill the pages of newspapers such as the *Sentinel*, but Boston's biggest newspaper created a novelty of its own. During the 1930s, the *Boston Post* distributed canes to towns all across Massachusetts, one each per town to be given to the oldest resident. (Franklin still has its Post cane which is granted, ceremonially, to the town's oldest inhabitant, although it remains on permanent display at the Franklin Historical Museum.)

One of first Franklin recipient of the Boston Post cane was Mr. Clark, a 90 year old Civil War veteran, and one of the last local members of the GAR. Even in 1930, around half a dozen Civil War veterans were still living in town.

Four years into the Great Depression Franklin got a boost from Franklin D. Roosevelt's election. During the worst year of the Depression, 1933, Roosevelt enacted new programs to help unemployed Americans.

Starting in March, the federal government began to invest in Franklin. Washington's first move was to buy land at the corner of Dean Avenue and Main Street, from the Ray family and the Y.M.C.A. to build a new post office. The prime real estate cost only 17,000 dollars in 1933 money. In April, locals worked to reopen the Franklin National Bank that had closed its doors as a result of the economic crisis. By July, 300 people had been put back to work in local mills and factories. Even more federal aid came toward the end of the year. A huge engineering grant was given to the town, including plenty of money to fight gypsy moths. The gypsy moth superintendent was able to hire 20 men to help him clean up local orchards.

As Roosevelt expanded his programs, the number of people working on government projects slowly grew. After the Ray family donated a small pond right off of West Central Street, the town went to work building a public pool. Ford's pond was fed by Beaver Brook, which today still runs near the high school, beneath the Vendetti auto dealership, and by the Shell station. Members of Works Project Administration dammed up Beaver Brook, and built concrete bathhouses, opening the pool for public use.

Santina Crawford (born Accorsi and better known to friends and family as Sandy), a school girl at the time, remembers Ford's pond as a creepy place, covered in tangled vines, and inhabited by snakes, 'suckers,' and enormous snapping turtles. The suckers—some three feet long—migrated up the stream each year to breed.

Another project got underway after the Franklin Business Association joined the newly formed Rod & Gun Club to push for a 1000 acre game preserve in western Franklin. The proposal for Forge Hill (later Franklin) State Forest was quickly pushed through, and a huge property was bought up by the government. The land had poor soil, bad for farming, and served a better purpose putting people back to work.

The Civilian Conservation Corps, a military-styled civil works service, set up a camp on the top of Forge Hill. Two hundred and fifty

CCC volunteers poured in from across the country, building seven buildings in only a few weeks. Twenty two uniformed men staffed the camp, working to reforest Forge Hill and the surrounding area. Others headed out in truck 'caravans,' to spray creosote on trees as a defense against gypsy moths.

Roosevelt's programs put some people back to work, but unemployment continued to be widespread. After the end of prohibition, people could not make as much money bootlegging. Some turned to other illegal activities, such as burglary.

Florence Cherington, was alone in her large home on Chestnut Street one evening when her dog began barking at an intruder in the yard. Grabbing a rifle, she waited to see what would happen. In spite of two bright lamps lighting up the yard, the burglar still decided to smash a window on the ground floor. Florence fired her rifle out the window, but the burglar dodged out of sight, just in time and ran off. As the *Sentinel* noted "...That man might right now be adorning the cold slab in a Franklin undertaker's room."

Some crimes committed to makes ends meet were simply bizarre. In one case, the Franklin police arrested a man accused of stealing a 750 pound electric motor from the Greene icehouse on Washington Street, single handedly. The man confessed to the crime. In a different situation, described by the *Sentinel* as, "...probably the strangest case of attempted extortion ever recorded in police annals," a letter was sent to the chief of police threatening acts of arson, kidnapping, and assassination, targeting the police unless 5000 dollars was left at a well on Indian Rock. The case was so bizarre, that the chief of police called in the FBI.

Strangest of all, was the removal of an *entire* bridge, with an acetylene torch. The North Bellingham road, across Mine Brook, was closed due to damage in the 1938 hurricane. As the causeway and bridge fell into disrepair, it was neglected by the town until one day, when a hunter discovered that the bridge was missing!

The police caught up with Lawrence Desjarlais of Bellingham, and arraigned him in district court. Desjarlais claimed he was no criminal—he figured that since the bridge was abandoned, the scrap steel could be melted down and used by the military. Still, he was roundly criticized by everyone for removing the remains of the bridge.

Attempting to use worker discontent to their advantage, out of town labor organizers, and roaming strikers from other communities poured into town from time to time. In September, 1934, they came in such large numbers that mills (except for Clark, Cutler, McDermott) were closed, and employees kept home by mill owners eager to avoid strikes.

For all the money that the government invested in public works, most people during the '30s were forced to get inventive. As a girl, Sandy Crawford remembered the haphazard building style common amongst her neighbors on West Central Street. Whenever people happened upon building supplies they would add a little bit onto their house. Because hardly anyone could afford new boards, paint, or other basic supplies, houses had their own eclectic appearances. One of her family's neighbors built a house without a basement, leaving it up on blocks—he finally dug a basement when the economy improved.

One of the few businesses actually growing, was the salvage industry. The US government and Japan were buying up scrap metal by the ton—much of this metal would later be used to build weapons in World War II. Families doing everything possible to save money, saw scrap metal as a fine way to earn a few extra dollars that could be used to pay for food, clothing, housing and other basic necessities. The many town dumping sites that Edward Wilder had once fretted over became a boon for local families. Adults and children picked over the dumps, collecting every bit of useful scrap metal that they could lay their hands on. Each metal and alloy commanded a different price.

Some metals such as brass and aluminum were particularly prized, but even common steel, iron, and even cardboard were worth money. Children filled their heads with the latest scrap prices, and many were able to recite the latest values for each metal. Once a family had collected enough scrap, one of the local junkmen would come to buy a load from them. The Garelick and Sullivan family (competitors in the dairy business) competed with one another to become major junk dealers in the area. One of the Garelick brothers ran a successful salvage operation selling the scrap metals that he bought from families to the US government, which sold much of the scrap metal to Japan, in turn. The Garelicks ended up leading the Sullivans when fire claimed the Sullivan truck and salvage shed.

Collecting scraps became almost a local pastime, especially for children. The most exciting thing that West Central Street kids could think of was visiting one (or both) of the dumps on Beaver Street, near Beaver Pond. One was located roughly where the Chelsea Drum Company is today, while the other was across from the current soccer field. These dumps were crammed with old cans, rusting chassis, bedsprings, just about everything, in fact. There were always surprises for the neighborhood children when they went scavenging. One time, Sandy and her friends discovered several boxes of chocolates that had turned *white* with age. They were delicious, just the same. On another occasion, the children stumbled on a large crate full of eggs. Eggs were sometimes a rare commodity, and the kids were all looking forward to enjoying them, until one egg fell out of the crate and shattered on the ground. The smell was awful! Beyond a doubt, these eggs were deadly. With typical pragmatism, the kids went ahead and pelted each other with volleys of stinking, rotten eggs. The slimy yolks and whites were all over Beaver Street, and all over their clothes. Everything stank. But by the end, they were grinning like maniacs.

Sandy, a witness to the CCC activity in Franklin experienced the Great Depression first hand. Like so many others, her family often struggled to make ends meet when jobs dried up. Her father, Mr. Accorsi, was no stranger to hard work. Unfortunately, as Sandy recalls, her father spent most of 1930s in semi-retirement. He was losing his sight and slowly going blind. Despite his condition, Accorsi found every opportunity to earn money for his family. At the Franklin rail yard, he worked unloading coal gondolas. The other men at the yard were well aware of his failing sight, and let him unload a gondola single handedly (rather than involving the two or three laborers usually used to unload coal) so that he could earn more money for his work. In addition to unloading coal, Accorsi was a Work Projects Administration man, laying pipes underneath the streets of Franklin.

As if the '30s were not already bad enough, one of the worst hurricanes in New England history struck in 1938. The hurricane swept away entire communities in Rhode Island, toppled tens of thousands of trees, and did a great deal of damage in Franklin. Locally, high winds toppled the Dean Academy bell tower, and destroyed the Baptist church steeple (and the rest of the church with it). The destruction of the Baptist church actually worked out well for everyone—the Baptists and Congregationalists merged to become the Federated church.

Meanwhile, events in Europe were taking a turn for the worse, and a generation hardened by financial catastrophe would have to prepare to face wartime hardships ahead.

In the early 20th century trolleys, and later buses and cars carried locals to amusement parks and dance halls at almost every little lake and pond. Lake Pearl Dance Hall (above, in Wrentham) was particularly popular, and closed only for the 1918 flu epidemic. (Courtesy of Franklin Public Library)

Even as many students left for wartime service, Dean Academy still put together a good football team in 1918. Dean football and baseball were closely followed, along with other amateur teams such as the Clar-Macs, and Benny's Oilers. (Courtesy of Franklin Public Library)

In search of local spectacle, it appears that the owners of a tower on East Central Street may have decided to open up to the public offering a bird's eye view of the town, like the one in this postcard. (Courtesy of Franklin Public Library)

As one of the largest towns in Norfolk County, Franklin hosted many events—often parades—to celebrate holidays, enlist voters for a candidate, and so forth. Here, a troop of cavalry marches through the downtown, around the time of the Spanish American War. (Courtesy of Franklin Public Library)

More genteel than some sports, golf came to Franklin with the formation of a country club in the 1890s, a new golf club and clubhouse were built in the '20s. (Courtesy of Franklin Public Library)

Appealing to a different audience than football or baseball, tennis appears to have attracted both men and women spectators and players to Dean's courts. (Courtesy of Franklin Public Library)

These female athletes appear to be playing basketball, most likely at Dean Academy. Notice that the players are wearing baggy pants rather than cumbersome dresses, suggesting that the photo was probably taken in the '20s.

The original YMCA in the downtown had its tennis courts purchased by the federal government to build a new post office in 1934.

Stanley Chilson: Photographic Fanatic

Stanley Chilson, master gardener and local photographer, spent more than 30 years recording almost every aspect of Franklin life through moving and still pictures. In addition to his many movies of Franklin life, Chilson's fire photos, showing the work of the Franklin Fire Department, offer a unique look at everyday life, and the wild disasters that sometimes hit townspeople. The following images, courtesy of the Franklin Historical Commission, are a tiny sample of Chilson's work, showing some of the typical calls the fire station received in the 1930s.

Police Chief Knowlton (center) looks as if he's missed his morning coffee, as he inspects the damage done by a fire at the Cornwall house on March 21. Note the two at center right sharing a cigarette. Apparently one fire wasn't enough for them.

On December 2, 1938, someone seems to have taken an order for roast chickens too seriously at E.B. Parmenter's henhouse on King Street.

In comparison to today's 4th of July fireworks, there is no comparison! In the '20s, '30s, '40s, and later, a massive tower of tar-soaked railroad ties was erected each summer and lit on fire, creating the mother of all bonfires.

Chapter 15:

The Fight of a Generation

...The High School physical education program stressed combat readiness. Boys were taught "commando" tactics by Howard Landry, the PE teacher, and how to march in step...

The head of the Forest Fire Department was grateful. The soft, green and white wood of the trees downed during the hurricane had been too damp to catch fire. The threat of fire had passed, and now the work of clearing away the trees was well underway. Homeowners dug out their saws and axes, slowly but surely turning a fire hazard into firewood. The Works Projects Administration men were busy building sidewalks, extending water mains, trimming trees, and spraying arsenate of lead onto town shade trees in the endless war on gypsy moths. The Board of Health had as much reason as the head of the Forest Fire Department to be thankful. A serious outbreak of rabies during the summer of 1939 had been dealt with, and nobody had been infected, all though two people had been bitten. Matters had become so desperate in the hot summer of '39 that a town-wide restraining order had been in place for pet owners. Dogs were not to leave houses and yards, and could be put down if the health inspectors saw fit.

The early '40s saw the slow winding down of the Great Depression. The WPA still had 23 men on the payroll, and the town still spent heavily on the poor farm. Surplus goods were given out by the government all around town—everything from lard and prunes, to girls' bloomers.

As the new war in Europe increased in intensity, one lazy summer passed into the next in Franklin. Students took radio classes, and played softball against City Mills at Fletcher Field; average people could afford to ignore the war, and focus on other things. But the war was becoming harder to ignore. In early 1941, a local Civilian Defense Committee was set up, to prepare the town for air raids. An academy trained volunteers to manage an emergency call center, and to act as air raid wardens trained in first aid. Even Boy Scouts joined in the effort, training to send messages by carrier pigeon, while school administrators designated air raid shelters for their students.

President Roosevelt initiated a peacetime draft, and 750 men turned out to register for Selective Service. The government stepped up defense preparations. Locally, the idea of war still seemed distant, but people were beginning to change their mindsets. A community rifle range was proposed by the selectmen, but in lieu of that, winter classes were held at the Rod and Gun Club's range to teach ordinary people how to aim and shoot firearms. Some people even proposed rebuilding Route 140 as a four lane military road extending to Camp Edwards on Cape Cod. The Wrentham, Franklin and Foxboro selectmen officially endorsed the idea, but nothing ever became of it.

Finally, on December 7, 1941, war finally came. Japan bombed Pearl Harbor and the US was thrust into the largest war in history. As young men and women from Franklin hurried to the nearest recruiting stations, or were summoned by the War Department, Civilian Defense stepped up its operation. By 1942, there were 75 volunteer telephone operators at the Report Center, 35 air raid wardens, and many others in the Red Cross or emergency services. Franklin had four blackouts in 1942 and six daylight air raid tests. Teachers were kept after school to study civilian defense handbooks, learning how to identify poison gases, how to operate pumps and how to deal with incendiary bombs.

Everyone cooperated. At the high school, a regimen of civics (and even religion classes) drove home American values; mathematics students enrolled in aeronautical engineering courses, to train for wartime work. Metalworking students learned how to operate precision machine tools at the Thomason Press Building, needed to build aircraft. Meanwhile carpentry students gave up on furniture, and made more than 120 detailed model airplanes to train pilots in aircraft identification. The federal government requisitioned type writers from the schools, and required that all school buses shorten their routes and carry Certificates of War Necessity (allowing a certain amount of fuel for each bus). Schools were used as meeting places as people gathered to register for sugar and gasoline rationing.

The police tracked down soldiers and sailors absent without leave, and purchased submachine guns and gas masks-- just in case. Franklinites bought war bonds, donated scrap metal, and contributed to the USO. The High School physical education program stressed combat readiness. Boys were taught "commando" tactics by Howard Landry, the PE teacher, and how to march in step. Many teachers left to serve, leaving the schools understaffed, but the students were more dedicated than ever before.

Civilian Defense turned into a competition between volunteers. Those who contributed the greatest number of hours were written up glowingly in the town report. The winner was certainly Svea Drolet--a volunteer telephone operator who contributed 618 hours for the war effort.

Most people took the idea of enemy attack very seriously, especially after they heard about a pleasure boat that sank mysteriously off the coast of Maine. Through the grapevine, people heard that the boat had been sunk by a German U-boat, 'proof' of enemy operations near at hand. Blackouts were strictly enforced and Franklin appeared as a ghost town each night. Somehow, the workers at the factories in Unionville found their way through the impenetrable darkness of Rt. 140 on foot.

German air raids on New England were actually impossible, despite all of the hype. The Nazis simply did not have any aircraft that could fly nonstop to North America and back, carrying a load of bombs. But in the uncertain days at the beginning of the war, anything seemed possible, and it seemed like a good idea to prepare for the worst. If nothing else, civilian defense reminded people that there was a war.

Most Franklinites did not need reminding. By war's end, more than 1000 local men and women were in the service. Civilian defense and air raids aside, rationing was a constant reminder of the day to day impact of the war on the home front. As a result of the gasoline shortage, many people turned to bicycles.

The police bike registry usually licensed about 100 bikes a year, but in 1943, the station was busy registering almost 600.

For a town with only a few thousand people, a large fraction of whom served in the military, able bodied workers were increasingly scarce. Many of the women who had not enlisted as nurses or other war workers took over vital jobs in Franklin and the surrounding towns. Sandy Crawford, after graduating from Franklin High in 1940, went to work at the Archer Rubber Company in Milford, making ponchos and rubber raincoats for use by troops in the tropics.

When the war came to an end in 1945, Sandy was laid off and her job was taken by a returning soldier. She heard from an aunt, living in Maine, that there were many jobs were opening up 'down east,' and headed north. She settled in Rumford, Maine, a major paper town in rural, western Maine. Rumford was full of opportunities for anyone willing to work hard. The city's mills had supplied millions of reams of paper that became service records and sortie reports, helping to drive the war effort. Sandy found a job at the Oxford Paper Company's mill, sorting creamy sheets of magazine paper, and checking them for quality. At the same time, a young US Army veteran named Howard Crawford was working in the shipping department.

Howard, unlike Santina, had lived his life in Maine. Born in Bristol, Connecticut, his parents moved the family to Maine when he was only two months old. Growing up during the Great Depression, Howard remembered his family moving about often. His father was an itinerant laborer for much of Howard's childhood. Traveling light, Howard's father would be gone for days, even weeks, traveling the roads of Maine in search of employment. Whenever he found a job, he would return to the place where his family was staying and tell them to pack their bags. The Crawfords could pack up all of their belongings and get on the road in only an hour or two.

As a kid, Howard did everything he could to bring in a little extra money for his family. In 7th grade, he found the rusty frame of a baby carriage, and put it to good use, going door to door to collect scrap metal. Half way through his sophomore year in high school, Howard's father handed him an axe, and told him to quit school. The two headed into the thick forests of Maine to harvest timber to feed the gluttonous paper mills and lumber yards all across the state. At different times, Howard joined other young men to tackle larger, more profitable salvage jobs than he had worked in the 7th grade. Paddling out into the middle of Maine's Kennebec River in rowboats, Howard and other men would attach chains and ropes to the many rusty car chassis that had been dumped in the river; raise them, and sell them to earn money.

In 1939, Howard put his logging skills to a new use. He joined President Roosevelt's Civilian Conservation Corps serving at first, in Aroostook County, an immense region of northern Maine. As a Maine CCC volunteer, Howard was in the minority, amongst the heavily accented Louisiana Cajuns that made up most of his formation. After serving in Aroostook County, Howard was sent to Westfield, Massachusetts to join in the war on gypsy moths. The CCC men in Westfield, like the volunteers in Franklin, tackled gypsy moths, by spraying trees with creosote.

When World War II broke out, Howard was still a member of the CCC. He decided that it was time to serve his country in a different way; so in 1942, he enlisted in the US Army. At least, he tried to enlist. Unfortunately, he was turned down by Army recruiters and listed as "Four-F" because of 'bad eyes.' In one eye his vision was poorer than the other, and he could only fire a rifle with his left hand. Howard bided his time, until 1943, when the US Army suddenly ran out of recruits and started calling up middle-aged men and those rated as "Four-F." This time, he was drafted. Howard's brothers were as eager as he was to enlist. His younger brother lied about his age, and ended up fighting on Iwo Jima at only 15 years old.

In Howard's mind, the Army was no different than the CCC. Enlisted men in both organizations wore uniforms and lived disciplined camp lifestyles.

After the war, Howard returned to familiar territory going to work in Maine. One day, after work at the Oxford Paper Company, Howard and one of his friends were walking down Rumford's main street when they spotted a young woman going into a jewelry store. Howard turned to his friend and said, "She looks like a farmer's daughter; I think I'll marry her." Never one to mince words, Howard took Sandy on a date that very same evening. He fulfilled his promise, too, and married her not long after.

The end of the war was one of the happiest times in years, for the first time since the 1920s people had more than just hope to carry them along. The economy was picking up, and putting people back to work. Many returning soldiers started new businesses. Maurice Herbert and Edward Monier decided to start a paint company. The two veterans took out a small bank loan, and bought the 5,000 square foot Whitney Worsted mill in Unionville and made it into the world headquarters of their venture--Franklin Paint Company. To start out with, they produced house paint and traffic paint for the roads. But, there was too much competition from the big house paint makers and they decided to focus on traffic paint alone. Almost 70 years later, Franklin Paint continues to churn out paint from its Franklin factory (now located off of Cottage Street). Wartime inventiveness led local plumber Joseph Daddario to start making his own sheet metal ductwork, for customers. After the war, he expanded this part of his business, creating Franklin Sheet Metal in 1948 on the second floor of his Dean Avenue shop. He turned repair work over to P.A. Polastri, and went into the wholesale plumbing supply business.

Some dreams were still too farfetched even at the end of the war. For example, a proposal to build a GM plant in town fell through, though a plant did end up in nearby Framingham. Even more farfetched was the idea of building the United Nations' headquarters in town! Catholic groups across Massachusetts dreamed of bringing nuns from Ireland to a new abbey in the US. This dream did come true in 1946 when Irish groups bought a huge property from the Garelicks on the Wrentham-Franklin line to set up the Mt. St. Mary's Abbey.

The birth of new factories and start-up companies helped to put returning soldiers back to work, reentering the civilian labor market. However, Franklin's future would be steered by a different group than the mill owners and industrialists. In Franklin, and in hundreds of towns like it across the country, local planning boards were about to engineer a very different future.

Chapter 16:

The Golden '50s

...A choosy homeowner could opt to build or buy an "Aloha," a "Middleville," a "Quebec," or one of the many other houses featured in the newspaper...

The jobs in Maine had dried up and the paper mills of Rumford were no longer running at full clip to satisfy military demand. Sandy Crawford was pregnant, and she and her husband Howard decided that it was time to search for greener pastures back in Massachusetts. Their life experiences mirror those of many other Franklinites at the time. In 1950, the Crawfords moved back to the family farm on Route 140 in Franklin. Howard went in search of work as soon as he arrived, but he found that jobs were still relatively few, even in Massachusetts. The job search had to be put on hold later that year when war broke out in Korea. America needed men right away to turn back the North Korean onslaught.

As a US Army reservist, Howard was called back to active duty. The same day that he boarded the Penn Central train from Franklin to Boston, heading east, Sandy was heading in the opposite direction to Milford Hospital to give birth to their son Michael. For the first 10 months of his life, Michael Crawford never saw his father. Howard, meanwhile, was part of a howitzer gun crew, taking part in the endless back and forth fighting across the Korean Peninsula (Howard had worked in a howitzer crew in World War II, facing fierce fighting at the Battle of the Bulge). More than a year after he shipped out, Howard was hit in the eye by a jagged piece of shrapnel. The US Army didn't have doctors skilled enough to treat the wound, and Howard was put aboard a transport and flown to Japan to have the shrapnel removed. He spent a month in Japan recuperating, before the Army doctors told him that as a reservist his one month stint in the hospital gave him a green light to go home. Howard headed back stateside to meet his son for the first time.

For returning Korean War veterans, like Howard, it was hard to find work. After his return to civilian life, he worked in jobs that ranged from agriculture and manufacturing to delivery. He delivered coal and heating oil with the Medway Oil Company, shoveling chunks of coal into burlap sacks, slinging them over his shoulder and hauling them down steep cellar stairs to keep customers warm through the winter.

Another job that Howard held was in Bellingham, where he worked for the Jones' family, who owned two dairy farms. He worked at both. Each morning he arrived at four o'clock a.m. to milk the farm's 40 cows. After the long business of milking was over, the cows were let out to graze while Howard and the other farm hands hayed in the fields. Late in the afternoon, the cows 'came home,' and it was time to repeat the milking process again. By early evening, Howard could finally drive back to Franklin. When he got home, it was time to help his father-in-law with farm chores and milk the family's small herd of dairy cows. By the time all of the farm tasks were done for the night, it was midnight, and Howard collapsed into bed to catch less than three hours of sleep before going back to work. Howard worked seven days a week for the Jones family, earning only 35 dollars each week for his work.

At different times Howard worked at Ketover's mill in City Mills, and at the American Felt Company in Franklin. His job at American Felt paid little and was grueling by any standard. In order to make felt, fibers were soaked and rinsed continuously, scrubbed and soaked in detergent, hammered and soaked again. Two burly men would take opposite ends of a sheet of felt, and pull in a tug of war to stretch out the fibers. The strenuous pulling and the endless exposure to detergent left Howard's hands bleeding by the end of a hard day at work.

Nonetheless, Howard was glad to have a job at the American Felt Company--every cent counted toward his growing family. Unfortunately, American Felt laid him off frequently, or suspended him when production was low, leaving him with no work at all. At one point, American Felt laid him off and Howard went in search of a new job. He turned up at Mendon Airport with 200 other men, all looking for work building a brand-new gas pipeline through Uxbridge and Mendon. The man in charge of hiring for the pipe laying company walked down the line of hopeful faces, handpicking men who he thought were up to the job. Howard didn't expect to be picked, but to his surprise, the manager picked him right away.

He went to work laying the pipeline. After the job was finished, the pipe laying company wanted him to head to Canada to build a much longer pipeline there. His manager told him that if he went to Canada, he would receive a handsome paycheck. Canada was only the beginning. His manager insisted that after Canada, the real money was to be found building pipelines in Saudi Arabia. As enticing as the high paying job was, Howard turned down the opportunity to work in Canada and Saudi Arabia, choosing to stay with his young family. At the same time, American Felt was picking up production and decided to rehire, with the promise that production would continue at a more even pace, and that they would not lay him off again. Two weeks later, the managers at American Felt broke their promise and Howard was without a job once more.

Forced to look elsewhere, Howard applied to work at a roofing paper factory in Walpole. While employment in Walpole was pending, Howard moved back up to Maine to work at a different paper mill. Besides spending days separated from his wife, and three young children, Howard's new job in Maine had a lot to recommend it. He worked in the bowels of the mill, supervising five boilers that kept the whole operation running. Thankfully, the boilers needed little attention. When they ran low on coal, all he had to do was a pull a chain to load them up with more fuel. Each Friday evening after five days watching the boilers, Howard would climb into his jalopy and drive hundreds of miles down the bumpy, narrow, winding back roads that were the only route to Franklin. At least his job at the paper mill was not as strenuous as his work for the Medway Oil Company, the dairy farms, or American Felt, but for a man like Howard, the long separation from his family detracted from the job's benefits.

At this point Howard got lucky, and was hired by Thomas McDermott the head of Clark, Cutler, McDermott. The year was 1957, and Thomas McDermott, a fellow Korean War veteran, hated to see a brother in arms without work. Clark, Cutler, McDermott was thriving, while American Felt was struggling to stay alive. At his new job, Howard no longer had to worry about the endless string of layoffs and rehiring that he had experienced at American Felt. Ironically, two days after he was hired by Thomas McDermott, Howard received a call from the roofing paper factory in Walpole, informing him that he had gotten the job. He chose to stick with Clark, Cutler, McDermott.

With a new, steady job in town, Howard was able to spend more time with his family. Although his children were still young, they had picked up his instinct for hard work. Michael Crawford, the oldest child, collected nightcrawlers from the garden to sell to the anglers headed to Beaver Pond. He also vended lemonade to sweat soaked Clark, Cutler, McDermott employees, towing his product in a toy wagon down the factory floor. Whenever Howard was away from the work, the family enjoyed life on the Accorsi farm, and the roadside attractions on Rt. 140—such as the miniature railroad where the Honey Dew shop is located today.

Throughout the 1950s, Howard had tried hard to get a job working for the Town of Franklin. His efforts had ended in frustration. His Korean War discharge record stated simply that he been discharged from the Army. The ambiguity of his discharge record--which wasn't explicit as to whether or not he was honorably discharged--was a sticking point for town officials. They refused to hire him unless he could prove that he had been honorably discharged. Finally, at the very end of the 1950s, Howard managed to convince the Town of Franklin of his good intentions, and that he *had* been honorably discharged. He was hired by the Highway Department. In another ironic twist, the School Department informed him two weeks later that they had hired him as well. As it turned out, Howard had applied for positions in both departments, but one had hired him first. It was time to make a decision. "This is an outdoor job, I like to work outdoors," Howard reasoned about his job with the Highway Department.

In between jobs, Howard made time to start the Franklin Little League with a group of other men. He also joined the Improved Order of Red Men (of which he is still a member). Back in the '50s, being a part of a group like the Red Men was almost essential; thousands of local members included store owners, farmers, and managers in charge of hiring and firing.

In part, the Crawfords had a difficult time during the 1950s because the US Army didn't bother to pay Howard's salary for three months, leaving his wife and young children to depend upon his father-in-law back in Franklin. The Crawfords were forced to sell their pickup truck just to make ends meet. For other folks, however, the 1950s were a more comfortable time. Franklin saw more new building than it had before. An aerial survey--the first conducted since 1936-- showed that all of Norfolk County had filled up. New houses were cropping up everywhere. The *Sentinel* chose to act in line with the Chamber of Commerce and the Rotary Club. Interspersed with Franklin and Norfolk County news were full page descriptions of affordable and fashionable ranch houses built in every shape and size imaginable. Each issue's featured ranch house had a different, fanciful name. A choosy homeowner could opt to build or buy an "Aloha," a "Middleville," a "Quebec," or one of the many other houses featured in the newspaper.

Men and women who served in the Korean War often missed out on the many opportunities at home. Although companies still laid people off frequently, jobs were much easier to find than in the '30s. For the first time in their lives, people in their 20s and 30s, starting families, could afford to buy new houses, cars, and even televisions. Because of a lack of money, most people had waited since the 1920s to look for new houses, and the demand for new homes was tremendous.

New construction followed new rules set forth by the Planning Committee. Real estate zoning—the new system--was designed to keep dirty factories away from residential areas, and encouraged builders to construct residential homes instead of barns and workshops.

Zoning became widespread across the US, in the years just before, and right after World War II. By designating land as residential, commercial, industrial, agricultural, or open, towns such as Franklin changed the way that people were allowed to build and settle. In towns across the country, thousands of acres of land became prime real estate for development into new homes. Add to that returning service members eager to start families, and subsidized government mortgages, and towns like Franklin had a real estate boom on their hands.

New families sought after houses that would be considered small by modern standards, often with only a quarter acre of land. But the small land area demands of prospective homeowners made it easier for developers to divide up properties into lots; some envisioned a suburb patterned after the famous Levittown community in Pennsylvania. Not all plans went ahead. For example, the area around Bright Farm (present day Village Plaza) is said to have been considered for a large neighborhood.*

During the Korean War, the luck of Franklin servicemen and women held. Not a single person was killed, although at least one soldier was seriously wounded by a grenade. For Congressman Martin, who represented Franklin and much of Norfolk and Bristol County in Washington, the 'Red' menace in Korea was doubly dangerous on the home front. Joe Martin hailed from North Attleboro, and by the 1950s had become the House Majority Leader. Martin had plenty of connections to people in high places. He was a good friend Senator Joe McCarthy whose 'witch hunts' are still infamous, as well as President Eisenhower. Throughout his career, Martin's connections paid off. During World War II, Martin's brother owned a filling station in Wrentham that never seemed to have any curtailments on its supply of gasoline despite nationwide rationing. Martin was a frequent feature in the *Sentinel*, espousing anti-communism, and discussing the threat of a war in Europe with the Russians. Plenty of Franklinites had a chance to meet with Martin when he toured his district each year, stopping at the post offices in every town.

Many people shared Martin's fears that communists were ready to overthrow the American government--or start a war-- with little or no provocation. Especially after Americans learned that the Soviet Union had built atomic bombs, these fears gained new credibility. Even with the Nazi threat gone for good, Franklin kept its Civil Defense Department alive. Rather than wait for a war to materialize, officials in Franklin prepared in advance. After attending a meeting of state civil defense officials in Brockton, Selectman Pond helped to draw up an emergency response plan. If a war scenario came about, the Franklin regular and auxiliary police would evacuate the town center and Route 140 in preparation for an attack. This was considered to be a 'yellow alert.' What followed would be a 'red alert,' at which point, everyone was advised to take cover, with only military vehicles allowed to travel on the

The area where Village Plaza is today was once a large, sandy hill used by Dean students for downhill skiing.

roads. The nightmarish view of an attack was not entirely farfetched. Located almost equidistant from Boston and Providence, Franklin might have experienced radioactive fallout if either city had been attacked by the Russians. Even Milford, Woonsocket, and Attleboro, prosperous manufacturing communities and major regional cities, were potential targets.

Oddly, it was not A-bombs, but hurricanes that gave the Franklin auxiliary police and civil defense volunteers their greatest test. In the summer of 1954, Hurricane Carol swept up the east coast, striking New England particularly hard. Franklin was spared the worst of the storm, but many houses lost shingles, and trees were downed all over town. The Dean campus was littered with branches that would have to be cleaned up. Carol was an unpleasant surprise, but did little lasting damage to Franklin. A year later, when Hurricane Diane swept north from the Caribbean it was a different story.

Diane was preceded by a weak hurricane dubbed Connie that dumped rain into rivers and streams all across New England. The waters in Mine Brook Pond, held back by an old wooden mill dam, rose rapidly. When Diane struck days later, there was simply too much water for the old dam to hold, and it failed. The failure may have been unspectacular, but it was very destructive. A torrent of water swept out of the flooded lowland area and raced toward Medway. Alongside Grove Street, the surging waters of Mine Brook knocked out the small dam at Golding's mill pond, adding more water to the flood, which swept over Grove Street carrying away all of the pavement. The churning waters swept past the town sewer beds, disappearing into the swamp surrounding the brook, ultimately reappearing in Medway to flood parts of the town center.

Franklin experienced power outages, and high waters flooded many citizens' basements. The *Sentinel* went out of print during the storm and its immediate aftermath, but it had plenty to say about the small disaster when its presses starting operating again on August 25. Medway had been hit the hardest out of all the communities neighboring Franklin. The flood waters from Mine Brook did combined damage with the overflowing Charles River. In one place, a bridge across the Charles River was washed out. Village Street, connecting Medway to Millis was under several feet of water, and there were concerns that the dam at Choate Park would give out. Medway residents assessed the storm as worse than the catastrophic Hurricane of 1938.

Even the Medway Pumping Station came under threat of flooding from the waters of the Charles River, and volunteers from Franklin were called in to help the town out of a difficult situation. Driving down Bent Street, in Franklin, with a 30-ton bulldozer in tow, Henry Zide was bound for Medway to help with the relief effort when the brakes of his tractor gave out, sending him careening downhill. A Medway patrolman and selectman trailing him in a police car watched in astonishment as Zide steered his runaway vehicle into a tree, rather than the Charles River, jumping out at the last moment. Zide came very close to becoming the only local casualty of the storm, but managed to escape unscathed, along with the bulldozer. His truck was not as lucky.

An astonishing total of 12.68 inches of rain fell on Franklin during Hurricane Diane. Thankfully, no lives were lost in the storm. The only casualties in the 1954-'55 hurricanes were two local civil defense volunteers who forgot to wear slickers while patrolling in the high winds and rain, who came down with pneumonia. Together, Franklin and Medway suffered tens of thousands of dollars in damage from Hurricane Diane.

Sadly, the victims of a fire in December 1954 were not as lucky as the many residents who experienced the back-to-back hurricanes of the '50s. The tragic story was picked up by the Associated Press, and printed in newspapers as far away as Maryland. Reginald DeBaggis, a polisher at an Attleboro jewelry plant, was lucky to make it out with his life, managing to save his wife and six month old daughter when an oil stove exploded, starting the midnight blaze. The fire claimed the lives of five DeBaggis children trapped in the house. Reginald, his wife, and their youngest child had been sleeping on the ground floor, while the five older children had been sleeping right above the kitchen where the fire began. The fire tore through the warm, dry farm house. DeBaggis rushed back inside, but the flames had all but consumed the stairway leading to the second floor. Trying desperately to rescue his children, DeBaggis raced around the house breaking windows, hoping to get inside. But each time a window dissolved into shards, flames came billowing out. DeBaggis suffered numerous cuts and was badly burned, but his attempts at rescue all failed. The DeBaggis farmhouse fire ranks as one of the single deadliest disasters in Franklin history.

In spite of such disasters the '50s were the best of times for Franklinites, including Franklin's young people. Franklin High School resembled a regional high school, serving many towns nearby that were even smaller than Franklin. Students came from Bellingham, and sometimes even from as far away as Walpole.

Marlon Brando-style macho fights were not uncommon at the Nautilus Restaurant, opposite the fire station, downtown. For teens in the late '50s, the Nautilus was the place to be, while for town officials and parents the restaurant stood out as a public nuisance. Fights between gangs of young men from Franklin and Milford broke out almost every night, in spite of the police cruiser usually stationed at the front door. One of the fiercest public meetings in history was held to consider the restaurant's request to renew its juke box license!

A popular attraction in the '30s was the Indian Rock farm where the Horace Mann Plaza is today. Out for a day's ride on the pony track are two teenagers, identified as Donald (left), 15, and Stanley (center), 17.

Taking off on September 30, 1930, the airship *Neponset* took Franklinites on a half-hour airborne journey above the town to attract customers to Simon & Sons Furniture.

Although the poor farm at Uncas Pond dated from the mid-1800s, it saw continued use into the 1940s, as Franklin's poor—particularly the elderly—sought a means of support. Residents grew much of their own food, and received government surpluses to meet their needs.

A typical '20s house is dwarfed by a fallen tree, one of the tens of thousands knocked down by high winds during the Hurricane of '38.

As `38 Hurricane clean up gets underway, no load is too much for this sturdy truck, not even this enormous stump.

Heaps of snow hint at how much has fallen in the 1940 Valentine's Day storm. In the right side of the image is the current post office (built 1934). The earlier post office is the three story building at the end of the street.

In preparation for air raid injuries, Civil Defense volunteers blanket and bandage 'casualties' as part of a drill.

Franklin's mill landscape remained active during the '30s, such as these mills along the tracks by Union Street. However, at different points, strikes and unrest led to closure of factories. Wartime blackouts made it very difficult for workers to get home from work after hours.

Sponsored by the Work Projects Administration to put local men back to work, the town pool was built on Ford's Pond (behind the present day police station) by damming Beaver Brook. It remained open until 1982, when the Beaver Pond became the sole public swimming area. (Courtesy of Franklin Public Library)

The Franklin A&P grocery store pictured here in 1937.

Main Street, around 1950 is bustling with cars on a regular business day. Note the Stop and Shop supermarket on the right.

Another view of Main Street from the mid-1950s shows the view looking toward Clark Square. The Post Office is visible on the extreme left. (image courtesy of Franklin Public Library)

An aerial view of Garelick Farms, probably from around 1960. (image courtesy of Franklin Public Library)

The Benny's Oil Service "fleet" is pictured here around 1960.

Chapter 17:

Agriculture `Buys the Farm'

...At one point, Ernest Parmenter's hens held a world record for egg laying. At a competition in Rhode Island, his birds weighed in as the third most efficient egg layers in the world...

People in eastern Massachusetts enjoy fresh produce from farms. Farmers markets, harvest festivals, and farm stands always draw plenty of visitors, stocking up on sweet corn, apples, pumpkins, or eggs. Unfortunately, the few farms that remain in eastern Massachusetts are, for the most part, hardscrabble truck farms, that barely survive on annual sales of fresh vegetables. The food that Franklinites eat today was grown far away, not only out of state, but as far away as Canada and Mexico. As a result, most Franklinites today would be hard pressed to name the farm where their food originated. Not so fifty years ago. Fifty years ago, farming was a great way to earn an honest living, and Franklin was a visibly agricultural place.

In the early 1930s, about a dozen years after Edward Wilder toured Franklin dairy farms, most farmers still sold their milk to the big Boston distributors. Some things had changed in the farming business; for example, farmers were more likely to pasteurize their milk than they had been in 1917. As usual, the New York, New Haven & Hartford milk trains sped through the pre-dawn darkness bringing their precious cargo to the sleeping city dwellers miles away. Although trucks were becoming much more common, trains carried more milk than at any time in the earlier part of the 20th century.

Elm Farm, the Ray family's dairy in Unionville, had operated since the late 19th century. By 1931, the Rays were losing their place as the wealthiest and most charitable family in Franklin, as the town began to move away from many of its older industries. As a result, the Rays put Elm Farm on the market in 1931. Before long, two prospective buyers were looking eagerly at the beautiful property. The buyers were Max and Israel Garelick, two Russian-Jews who had immigrated to the United States, and settled in Woonsocket, around 1900. Israel had become an entrepreneur and a self-made man from a young age, saving up to purchase one dairy cow. As a young man, he was often seen traveling up and down the roads, doing business with farmers in Bellingham and Woonsocket. He sold his first cow, and bought another one, and another, and another, until he could afford to buy a pick-up truck. Israel's business skills paid off, and along with his brother, he was able to make a down payment on the Elm Farm in 1931. For the first time, the Garelicks had a farm all their own.

With the launch of their dairy enterprise, the Garelicks followed the trend of other Franklin farmers, selling their milk to the big distributors. Israel, always entrepreneurial, traveled hundreds of miles by road and rail, meeting with breeders in New York and Vermont to buy new, more productive dairy cows. It was not long at all before the Garelicks had a herd of 1,000 cows.

Max and Israel shared the former Ray mansion. One floor was set aside for each brother and his family. From time to time, other relatives lived in the wings of the mansion. The nine Garelick children enjoyed life on the farm, surrounded by family. The Garelick women made root beer and doughnuts for the family, and did office work, while the men tended to the cows. Max usually stayed home and managed the farm, but Israel would sometimes skip cattle shows to assist in the birth of a calf. Many hired hands and their families lived in apartments on the property while single workers lived in a boardinghouse, their meals taken care of by a full-time housekeeper.

The Garelicks may have owned one of the larger dairy farms in town, but they did not have a monopoly on the business. Harry Prince, the closest neighbor to the Garelick farm owned a sizeable herd that he grazed near where the BJ's plaza is today. In fact, the largest dairy in Franklin covered 250 acres and was owned by the Sullivan family off of Washington Street. Even the Sullivans were outdone by the Daniels family that had lived in Franklin since before the American Revolution. Luther Daniels owned a 300 acre farm with fields on both sides of Pond Street. Daniels raised dairy cows, as well as chickens and hogs. His hog barn and chicken barn were side by side, near the present day Tri-County property. The Daniels' property stretched from close to West Central Street all the way to the present day golf course on the Franklin-Bellingham line. The property sloped gently down to the swamps around Mine Brook. Daniels never extended fences down to the swamp, and cows often wandered across Mine Brook and into Bellingham.

Alongside the Daniels farmhouse stood a two-story wooden barn that housed the herd during inclement weather and after dark. At one point, Luther Daniels was told bluntly by a health inspector, to move his milking operations someplace else. New regulations dictated that cows could not be milked in a barn with a wooden floor, because the pores in the wood might become a refuge and breeding ground for the deadly, milk-borne disease listeria. As a result, Daniels built a more modern, single story milking barn, with a concrete floor, that still exists today.

Luther Daniels would slowly sell off parcels of his farm to become houses, streets and roads, but also farms. In the early 1950s, Daniels sold 125 acres to the Compton family from Dorchester. The Comptons owned a company that installed sprinkler systems in commercial buildings, but they soon became interested in horses. Starting out with only a few ponies, the family became very enthusiastic about horses and horse racing. While briefly pursuing horse racing, the family built a single story stable. They rented out space in the new stable for boarders, and turned their 125 acres into a horse farm, frequented by Dean College students interested in riding. With their purchase from Daniels had come the Daniels hog barn and chicken barn, both of which saw extensive use in addition to the stable.

Starting in the mid-1960s, the Comptons set their sights higher, starting up a side-business, as horse transporters. By 1969, hard work and business sense paid off--they owned eight semi-trailers, and employed two full-time mechanics to keep the trucks running. They bought two other horse transportation companies, a business in Foxborough and another in Georgia. As the company grew, and acquired more transportation permits, they were able to operate in 29 states, by 1979.

The Comptons hauled race, polo, hunting and show horses around the Northeast and the eastern United States. The business was a demanding one. Often, drivers were forced to get under way by four o'clock in the morning in order to reach stables and load up their equine passengers before dawn. The two busiest days of the year were Thanksgiving and Christmas day, when many riders took their horses on enormous hunting excursions. When they were not on the highway, the Comptons sometimes kept horses in fields along Pond Street. Once in a while, rusty horseshoes still turn up in yards that were once horse pastures. The demand for professional horse transporters lessened after deregulation in the '80s and the business became extremely competitive, convincing the Compton family to pull out. In the early '80s, they sold the last of their horse pastures on Pond Street, for development into Overlook Drive.

The clucking of chickens and the crowing of roosters was almost as loud as the lowing of cows in the 1930s, '40s, '50s, and early '60s. As with milk, city dwellers demanded plenty of chicken and eggs to satisfy their voracious appetites. All throughout eastern Massachusetts, long, shingled chicken barns sprang up supplying eggs for the breakfast table, and whole chickens for the dinner table. The shrink wrapped Purdue chicken that everyone is familiar with today was still in the future, when Franklin chicken farmers were at their peak. Chicken barns, like cow barns, were everywhere in town. Some were located on Maple Street, others on Prospect and Washington, but the largest cluster was around the present Parmenter school. The Parmenter family owned some of the largest chicken barns, some three to four stories high.

At one point, Ernest Parmenter's hens held a world record for egg laying. At a competition in Rhode Island, his birds weighed in as the third most efficient egg layers in the world.

The Parmenters were known regionally, and around the world for their own variety of the famous Rhode Island Red--the Parmenter Red. The rust-colored Rhode Island Red is known to farmers as a hardy, docile breed, laying hundreds of eggs a year. The Parmenter Red improved on some of the qualities of the Rhode Island Red, gaining a good reputation with farmers. As a result of its reputation, and the fact that the Parmenters were the originators, and primary breeders of the variety, Franklin became a hub in the chicken trade.

The Railway Express Agency (a major package shipper before FedEx and UPS) owned a depot alongside the rails on Union Street. Into the '50s and '60s, REA shipped 10,000 newly hatched Parmenter Red chicks each week through the Franklin depot, bound for farms around the country and around the world. In a single year, as many as half a million Parmenter Red chicks may have been shipped through the REA depot.

Even farmers operating on a much smaller scale than the Parmenters were able to turn a profit. One man named Baddarian living near the Garelick farm found new uses for his older chickens, during the Great Depression. Each Sunday morning after church, he sold roasted, barbecued, and fried, half-chickens to churchgoers driving back to Bellingham, through Unionville. Even families struggling to make ends meet could afford Baddarian's roasted chickens.

At one point in the late '30s, a poultry company from Worcester tried to set up operations in the old Appleton rubber plant. Their planned slaughterhouse was intended to butcher 8000 hens per day that would then be seasoned, and packed into refrigerated trucks for the journey to the upscale markets of New York and Philadelphia.

Piggeries were as common in Franklin as dairy and chicken farms. Franklinites living all over town raised pigs, but the biggest single pig farm was located on Lincoln Street, surrounding the Dacey family's swampy dairy farm. The huge Lincoln Street piggery was owned by the Garelicks. The Garelick piggery was home to literally thousands of pigs.

Pigs were usually fed household scraps, helping to get rid of home garbage. Food scraps were collected around town twice weekly, boiled, and fed to pigs.

When pigs were fat enough, they were sometimes slaughtered locally and certified by the town's Slaughtering and Dairy inspector, much the same as Wilder witnessed in 1917. More often, though, pigs would probably have been slaughtered in large abattoirs in Brighton, Massachusetts, or turned into hot dog ingredients at a factory in Holliston.

Thomas Barnicle, a different type of local entrepreneur, decided to launch the Thomas Barnicle Macaroni plant in 1962, on Grove Street (where a self-storage company is located today). Barnicle bought all sorts of complicated equipment for his start up pasta factory. Unfortunately, the equipment was often poorly matched, and once a batch of pasta batter had been prepared there was no stopping the process. As the pasta machines extruded box loads of rigatoni and macaroni, Barnicle was busy trying to unload the stuff. He simply could not sell it fast enough. Instead, he found a novel solution. He would get local farmers to load dump trucks full of extra pasta to haul off. The pasta could then be soaked with a garden hose and fed to pigs. The pigs must have appreciated the new diet!

Keeping farmers supplied with feed grain, implements, and other equipment was an industry unto itself. The block in downtown Franklin that is now occupied by Dean Bank was occupied by Cataldo's Hardware. In addition to the usual tools such as hammers, saws, and screwdrivers, Cataldo's marketed a range of chicken care products and a variety of chicken feeders and waterers. Cataldo's Hardware shared space with a barbershop on the ground floor, and the local office of Worcester County Electric Company on the second floor.

Beside the REA depot on Union Street, the Agway that Franklinites visit today to stock up on insecticide and potting soil, did not exist. In its place, was a branch of Eastern States an agricultural supply store. Competing with Eastern States was a branch of Worthmore Grain, a company that sold feed grain, on Depot Street. Other people invested in agricultural improvements such as artesian wells, a niche filled by the W.S. Wyllie company in south Franklin.

Of course, the Garelicks, the Sullivans, the Daceys, and the Parmenters were not the only families involved in farming. The same entrepreneurial spirit that drove small business owners such as Cataldo and Wyllie to succeed was evident in many truck farmers around town, with small herds, small fields, and tremendous work ethic. Just like the big farmers, most of these resourceful truck farmers were eventually swept away in the '80s and '90s, but a few managed to hang on.

Akin-Bak farm* is one such truck farm. Sandy Crawford's father purchased the farm on Route 140 in 1938. He dug an irrigation pond (stocking it with hornpout that still live there today), planted crops, and bought cows. Israel 'Izzie' Garelick, the co-founder of Garelick Farms was a good friend of Mr. Accorsi. Sandy recalled "Izzie" dropping by, oftentimes to dicker with Accorsi about the price of his five dairy cows. To anyone unaccustomed to their endless wagering, it seemed that the two men were arguing, but it was all part of the act.

When Howard and his wife moved back to the family farm in 1950, they were short on everything but enthusiasm. Their original kitchen furnishings consisted of a table and chairs improvised from orange crates.

As Howard struggled to find work as far away as Maine, Accorsi managed the farm. He did not lack helping hands. Everyone helped out, including his grandchildren.(Howard Crawford was later inspired by his children's complaints about hard work on the farm to name the property "Aching Back." When he decided to put it on the sign, there was too little space for all of the letters, so he shortened it to Akin-Bak.)

The Crawfords raised livestock and grew a wide range of crops on their land. At different times, they owned not only dairy cows, but also ducks, chickens, pigs, a lamb, and a ram. Each year, they planted five acres with beets, cucumbers, lettuce. An entire acre was given over to tomatoes. What the Crawfords grew they sold. For years, the family ran a small vegetable stand in the yard in front of their house, where passing motorists could stop to buy fresh vegetables at a reasonable price. Vegetables were not the only things that they sold. The family would plant as many as 5,000 gladiola bulbs each year. When they sprouted, the proud, white flowers grew waist high. The Crawfords cut the gladiolas and sold them at their farm stand. Route 140 was the main route to get to Milford Hospital, and brilliant gladiolas from Akin-Bak farm brightened hospital wards two towns away.

When Accorsi bought the land in 1938, the property was advertised for 12 acres. One year, the property unexpectedly dropped to 11 acres. For years, Mr. Accorsi, Howard, and Sandy had paid the taxes for part of their property, which is now the location of the Franklin Glass Company. It was on this one acre where they grew their tomatoes, each summer. Then, one year, other people came along claiming to own the land—producing papers to prove their ownership. As the new official owners prepared to move onto the property, they allowed the Crawfords to finish growing their tomatoes.

To plant and harvest more crops, the Crawfords ultimately invested in a tractor, and agricultural equipment. In the late '50s, they bought an Ohio-built, Case tractor from an elderly gentleman in Bellingham. They accumulated all sorts of attachments and add-ons for the Case, including a large harrow, a potato digger, a spike-toothed harrow, and a sprayer for applying pesticides.

In the early 1960s, Howard was mailed a Montgomery Ward catalog, advertising bees and beehives for sale. At the time, the family had just finished putting in apple trees, and Howard hoped that the bees might help them to harvest a bumper crop, pollinating the apple trees in their small orchard.* He went ahead, and ordered the bees. As Howard learned from his successes and failures in starting up his hives, he became a founding member of the Norfolk County Beekeepers Association.

While tilling his land, Howard sometimes became an accidental archaeologist. Mr. Van Leuwen, the owner of an inn across Route 140 was a long-time resident who had acquired knowledge of Franklin's history over the years. He told the Crawfords stories, that had been passed down and retold over the years, and filled them in on the history of their property. At one time, it had been one of the sprawling properties of the Thayer family; before that, it had been a pasture for the horses which drew the stagecoach. In fact, Van Leuwen told them that their driveway had once been the start of the main road from Franklin to Woonsocket. Van Leuwen, was no liar, as Howard discovered. Over the years, he uncovered many rusty horseshoes and even an Indian arrowhead on one occasion.

Lettuce, beets, and tomatoes were popular amongst passersby, but for the Crawfords, a different crop topped them all. When Mr. Accorsi first purchased the farm, there were three towering cherry trees growing in the yard. Each summer, when the cherries came into season, the family would pluck them from the tree to enjoy raw. There were plenty of cherries, and rather than watching them fall and rot, Accorsi picked buckets of them to make into cherry rum. His recipe would have turned a teetotaler ashen, but was wonderful for everyone else. By mixing high-proof alcohol with whole cherries, and leaving the mixture to sit, Accorsi produced an incredibly flavorful drink. According to Sandy, the family still has three gallons stored in their cellar. After World War II, with the looming threat of atomic annihilation, Accorsi stashed the rum away—if war came, the family could at least enjoy their final minutes. One of Howard's most pleasant memories of life on the farm is sitting on the front lawn, on a warm July evening, every year, picking the Nanking cherries from the branches right overhead, as 4th of July fireworks arced into the sky.

The extent to which Franklin was very recently a 'farm town' is amazing. Just as remarkable as its extent, is the fact that Franklin farming declined so rapidly. For the most part, Franklin lost its agriculture at the very end of the 1960s, although strong evidence of its presence existed well into the '70s and '80s. Thanks to I-495, agriculture in the region "bought the farm."

At one point, Howard worked with Cornell University to develop new apple varieties. Akin-Bak farm is home to a few unique hybrids found nowhere else in the world.

Life on a Franklin Farm
Images courtesy of the Crawford family

Pictured here in the fall of 1965, the Crawford family's stand at Akin-Bak Farm on Route 140 sold fruits, vegetables and flowers to passing motorists for years. The family continues to sell fresh produce and wildflower honey in the present day. Note the Esso filling station and tree lined roadway in the background.

Howard Crawford joined by his family, stands in a field of gladiolas. Planting thousands of bulbs a year, the Crawfords sold gladiolas for patients at Milford hospital.

A surveyor goes to work at one of Franklin's first supermarkets, the plaza known today for Liquor World and the Meat House. This photo was taken in 1962 when the plaza was first built across from Akin-Bak.

Seen here in 1962, the Texaco station – now Shell -- on Route 140 (next to Akin-Bak farm) served a new breed of American motorist. With gas costing only about 31 cents a gallon, anyone could afford a full tank.

Howard's father, James Crawford, tills a field of beans with the help of his granddaughter Betty.

There's nothing quite like riding around in style on a summer evening, especially when the ride is an old Franklin fire engine! The Crawfords briefly acquired the old engine around 1975.

Chapter 18:

The New Frontier

...One man, high up in the local civil defense administration built himself a fallout shelter in his A Street home, complete with radios and supplies to last through a crisis...

Earth shattering in more than one way, the construction of Interstate 495 took Franklin by storm. Massachusetts had started to build superhighways such as Route 128 and the Turnpike, as far back as the 1950s. The new, multi-lane highways helped to relieve congestion on old, windy state routes, and made traveling easier. During the '60s, the federal government followed suit building a system of interstate superhighways. Regionally, I-495 was a bit of a latecomer, built in the mid-1960s, after I-95, I-93, and the other highways around Boston were well established.

The new outer belt of Boston was planned to stretch from Salisbury to Wareham, a goal ultimately realized by builders. When designers looked at the stretch of I-495 between Milford and Plainville, they looked at potential sites for exit and entry ramps. Originally, they planned two interchanges in Franklin. One on-ramp, and one off-ramp. It is a good thing that this proposal was not pursued. Vehicles getting off at one ramp would have been forced to drive through residential areas, creating traffic jams and disturbing locals, to get back on the highway.

Even though the off-ramp, on ramp controversy was cleaned up in good time, the project itself took many years to reach completion. In fact, I-495 in its entirety was not completed for more than a decade, and the southern reaches of the highway were still being built in the 1970s and 1980s. The stretch from Milford to Wrentham took several years to build and cost millions of dollars. The path of the highway cut across Mine Brook, narrowly avoided Grove Street, and wiped out a small neighborhood where the Mobil station and the Franklin Office Park West are today. Grove Street, which had been resurfaced after the 1955 floods was torn up and moved several hundred feet to the west.

A total of about half a dozen houses were seized and demolished close to the current Franklin Village Plaza. On the opposite side of the new highway, the historic Oliver Pond house was nearly demolished. Luckily, many Franklin citizens were opposed to the demolition of the landmark house. None of them were more outspoken than James Johnston, Jr. a Franklin High graduate and FHS history teacher, who used the Pond house as a home and as an antique shop. Only a few hours before the house was set to be taken, Johnston turned up with papers that declared the Oliver Pond house a protected historical landmark—a step that protected the building from demolition. Franklinites rejoiced, but planners were forced to return to the drawing board, shifting the route of the highway a few hundred feet to the east.

Thanks to the quick work, the Oliver Pond house was saved, and became an informal house museum by 1965, receiving Scout groups and school students interested in learning about their town's colonial past.

The smooth, sandy path of the highway attracted plenty of locals, looking for a quick route to Bellingham. When construction workers were not looking, many people drove around the traffic barriers in trucks and cars. Some even took their horses out for a gallop on the future superhighway. As the Franklin section neared completion, work began further southeast in Wrentham. Literally tons of bedrock had to be cleared away to make a path for the highway. As huge amounts of dynamite were planted in boring holes, and set off, the earth shook in Franklin, rattling everything from plates to windows.

Ironically, even after I-495 was opened to traffic, few people took advantage of the new superhighway. Most people did not commute far, and continued to live in the towns where they worked; they had little reason to travel. Franklin had its own grocery stores, recreation areas and factories--there was no need to look any further. According to motorists who traveled on I-495, up until the early 1980s, a driver could go for an hour without seeing another car or truck. The highway was so lonely that the government put in emergency call boxes along its length, to help stranded motorists to get help. On the rare occasions that anyone traveled far from home (for example, going to see a Patriots game in Foxborough) they usually traveled by state routes such as Rt. 140.

Some of the few people leaving Franklin in large numbers were high school graduates. A few signed up for service in the Peace Corps, but many more were called up to serve in the Vietnam War. Franklin lost eight men in Vietnam, mainly during the fierce fighting of 1968.

During the '60s, the town civil defense program continued to welcome new members, fearful of a nuclear war. In 1962, when the Cuban missile crisis raised the threat of war to new heights, many Franklinites seriously considering constructing fallout shelters. In addition to the fallout shelters in the basements of most public buildings, volunteers encouraged their neighbors to build shelters and stockpile food. One man, high up in the local civil defense administration built himself a fallout shelter in his A Street home, complete with radios and supplies to last through a crisis. He put out the word publicly in the *Sentinel* that he was willing to give away fallout shelter plans to any interested persons.

Students attending college were usually exempted for a time from military service, and many students rushed to enroll. Dean College helped to put Franklin on the map. Students from around southeastern Massachusetts attended, and came to know Franklin a little better as a result. The Dean campus of the 1960s was different that the one we know today. Four barns still stood on the campus. In the 20th century, the barns had been converted for student use, housing art studios, the dining hall, a campus bookstore and post office and the "Corral"—a very hip student snack bar.

Dean was open to students of all religious backgrounds, not only Unitarian Universalists. Nonetheless, Unitarian Universalists (the two groups merged in the early '60s) attended services at the Grace Church. The First Universalist Society of Franklin had dwindled, until only a handful of members turned out for services in the mid-60s. The small congregation knew they could not hope to keep the aging church building in repair. Finally, in 1967, they decided that it was time to move out. The church building was given to Dean College, and was torn down one year later. In its place, the college put in its E. Ross Anderson campus library.*

A bad drought in the early '60s forced Franklin to declare a water emergency, and turn to the builders of the I-495 for help. Plans were circulated for a special emergency reservoir in swamp to the west of the new highway, with the steep slope of the highway's edge serving as a dam. The plan never went forward.** To give kids a chance to get away from the summer heat, the town pool offered lessons throughout the summer months, and local mothers maintained a wading pool at Fletcher Park.***

Things were changing for Franklin in the '60s, as a result of the new superhighway, and together with zoning and new construction was starting to look like an attractive place for newcomers to build a family.

*Both the Universalists and the Episcopalians moved from School Street to new churches on Pleasant Street, in the '60s.

**Another proposal floated for almost a decade, involved reestablishing Mine Brook Pond with a dam, in hopes that water seeping from the pond would replenish the town's plummeting water table.

***Getting to Fletcher Park could be pretty challenging. After a pack of two dozen dogs from a farm on Beech Street menaced kids, mothers called for a bus to get to and from the park.

Chapter19:

The 1970s

...The legislature agreed to make the seven-spotted ladybug the official insect of Massachusetts, and invited the kids behind the idea to dress up as their favorite bug and visit the statehouse for a televised meeting with the governor...

On a March evening in 1970, 60 Franklin officials, ranging from selectmen to committee members filed into the high school library. Over two hours later they emerged, having reached an agreement with executives from Honeywell, an electronics company that produced everything from thermostats to computers. At the time, Honeywell was one of the most significant producers of computers in the United States. In Massachusetts alone, Honeywell employed close to 11,000 people, almost all in the burgeoning computer industry. Surrounded by back issues of National Geographic and shelves laden with books, the most active citizens in Franklin had enticed Honeywell into building a factory in town.

Honeywell executives went on to explain their choice of Franklin, over North Attleboro, Wrentham and Plainville, several weeks later during a dinner event in Bellingham. Although the other towns further south had as much land to offer as Franklin, none of them were as willing to bow to Honeywell's interests. At the end of March, a town referendum had shown overwhelming support for Honeywell. Voters agreed that the town should revise its zoning policies to attract Honeywell, as well as offering town water and sewer connection for an enormous discount.

Honeywell planned to build a quarter million square foot facility on the Sullivan farm off of Washington Street, to manufacture central processing units. The Honeywell deal was the talk of the town, and merited many articles and frequent updates in the *Sentinel*. For instance, the *Sentinel* published a front page article entitled "Computers: Franklin's Bright Hope?" Honeywell would bring hundreds, if not thousands of new families to Franklin, a boon for business and town tax revenues. Already, swarms of educated adults had moved from Boston's crowded neighborhoods to Billerica and Lexington where Honeywell had opened new plants.

Change was in the air all throughout 1970, as Franklin geared up for the arrival of the Honeywell plant. Planners hired artists and architects to draw up plans for an impressive new municipal building planned with new tax money. For the first time, Franklin also began worrying about the local environment. Beaver Pond's shores were littered with unsightly trash, blown from the dump across Beaver Street. The Selectmen contemplated a new town skating rink, while 17 citizens signed a petition to rescue the Red Brick School from closure. In other news, Harry Bullukian passed away, leaving the Boston Post cane temporarily unclaimed, while, in an unusual story highlighted by the *Sentinel*, Paul Cataldo befriended two ducks in Medway by feeding them large helpings of dog food.

The *Franklin Sentinel* had grand visions of itself as a competitor to the *Attleboro Sun*, the *Woonsocket Call*, and the *Milford Daily News*. It touted itself as the newspaper of western Norfolk County and covered not only national news (sparingly) but news from towns such as Walpole, Medway, Foxboro, Wrentham, Norfolk, Millis, and others. News items included not only the construction of Schaefer (now Gillette) stadium in Foxboro, but also the building of a hospital in Norfolk, and the opening of ski season at Wrentham's Sweatt Hill. Unfortunately, by trying to cover so much ground, the *Sentinel* covered very little at all.

For reasons that are unclear, but probably related to a shakeout in the computer industry, Honeywell pulled out of the deal at the last moment, leaving the town 'high and dry' without its planned high-tech development.

Global events, namely the war in Vietnam and the growing environmental consciousness nationwide, were pivotal during 1970 and '71 in Franklin. Two hundred western Norfolk County residents marched from Wrentham to Foxboro Common shadowed by local police, to protest the Vietnam War. They held signs, collected donations for Vietnamese refugees, and listened to protest songs. Students headed in the opposite direction, marching from Franklin High School to Milford for peace.

Far closer to home than the war in Vietnam was an unexpected and virtually unnoticed battle in the skies over Franklin. In March 1970 an Eastern Airlines flight with 73 passengers aboard was making its final approach to Logan Airport when the shooting started at an altitude of 5,000 feet, right above Franklin. John DiVivo, a deranged New Yorker with a gun in hand, stormed into the cockpit and demanded that the plane fly east. A struggle ensued for the gun in which shots were fired. The 31 year old copilot, James Hartley was killed. Before wrestling the gun out of DiVivo's hands, and shooting his assailant three times, pilot Robert Wilbur sustained a bullet wound to each of his arms. The unconscious gunman lay on the floor as Wilbur piloted the airliner in to Logan, executing an emergency landing, in spite his wounds. This latter day Sully Solanberger was the hero of what may be the only violent crime ever committed in Franklin airspace.

Another unusual event of the '70s was the 'terrorist' training camp at Armenian-American Camp Haiastan on Summer Street. Armenian Secret Army for the Liberation of Armenia volunteers reportedly trained to use explosives and submachine guns against the Turkish government.

Across America, many of the same people who protested the Vietnam War were beginning to take interest in a different cause—fixing pollution. As Franklinites began to notice the scope of pollution in their town, they began to organize and take action to prevent it. The sewer beds at Mine Brook remained primitive in the 1970s, virtually unchanged since the days when Wilder toured them, and had become one of the town's worst polluters by the early '70s. An open sewer channel snaked from Beaver Street, through the future Village Plaza parking lot, and Office Park West, led to the sewer beds on Mine Brook. For decades, neighbors of the sewer channel had gone without complaint. Perhaps on hot summer days, a person might be able to smell the channel's contents, but most of the year it was a not a noticeable problem. The flow of waste through the channel was turned on and off, as the sewer beds filled to capacity, and the channel was sometimes cleared out by the DPW. The contents of the beds were then left to dry in the sun. After drying out and solidifying, men from the DPW's highway and sewer department came along with shovels, scooping out the waste, and loaded it onto trucks to take to the town landfill.

But Franklin's population growth was outstripping the sewer beds. By the early 1970s, so much solid waste was entering the sewer beds that it no longer dried completely. The DPW was forced to bring in payloaders and back-hoes to clean out the beds. The problems down at the sewer beds threatened not only the waters of Mine Brook, which was already staggering under the weight of decades of industrial pollution, but also the men who worked for the DPW. Howard Crawford was a veteran worker for the DPW by the 1970s, with more than a decade of service to the town. One day, while participating in one of the frequent clean ups at the Mine Brook sewer beds, a small amount of human waste got onto his hand. Just minutes before, he had pricked his finger on a tiny shard of broken glass-- enough to draw blood. Crawford almost died of hepatitis, and was placed in hospital isolation for days. Always a fighter, Crawford recovered, and after many more days spent recuperating, he was back on his feet and ready to go back to work. Even after he recovered, Crawford was prevented from ever donating blood again to the Red Cross for fear that he might pass along hepatitis to a blood recipient. He had donated blood since 1943, and was within one pint of his fifth gallon donated to the Red Cross. Crawford's greatest disappointment was not the symptoms of hepatitis, but the fact that he had not donated five gallons of blood, at which point he would have received a handsome button from the Red Cross as thanks.

Reports surfaced continuously in the *Sentinel* of a possible safe dumping area in Sheldonville, or a new sewage treatment plant. For the time being, these were just proposals, but Franklinites nonetheless turned out in force to mark Earth Day 1971 by raking leaves on the common and combing the shores of Green's Pond for junk. The editors at the *Sentinel* seemed to have a particularly hard time spelling Green's Pond. In the Earth Day report, they listed it as 'Greasy' Pond (which was probably pretty accurate), while on another occasion it was misspelled Griei's Pond. The town sign makers were having just as much trouble naming local streets. A sign for 'Cresent' Street was photographed and printed up in the *Sentinel*.

In fact, Green's Pond was a popular spot for winter ice skating in Franklin. Beaver Pond had not become the town swimming hole yet, and a series of cold, snowy winters created perfect conditions for winter sports. Starting around 1967 winter sports took off in Franklin with the construction of the Klein Innsbruck downhill ski slope. Before Klein Innsbruck, Franklinites could go downhill skiing at Wrentham's Sweatt Hill or at one of two competing ski areas on the slopes of Cumberland's Diamond Hill--Diamond Hill Reservation and Ski Valley.

Wrentham's Sweatt Hill already had a thriving ski community. Students and teachers at King Philip High School joined the local branch of the National Ski Patrol, spending snowy days clustered in the warmth of the smoky concessions stand, and riding the lifts to the top of the slope. Some even worked on setting up the Klein Innsbruck ski area in the southwestern corner of Franklin, very close to Woonsocket and South Bellingham.

Klein Innsbruck joined a legion of small downhill ski areas around New England. Skiing at local slopes was not only fun but cost effective, especially during the recurrent energy crises of the 1970s, and Klein Innsbruck drew skiers from all across Massachusetts, filling up 500 parking spots each weekend. Well-heated eateries such as Klein's Lounge and Rumpelstilskin's Fine Food and Spirits were an added draw for outsiders.

Just as the *Sentinel's* editors were in doubt about the spelling of Green's Pond, Franklinites were in doubt about the future of rail service to the town. The Massachusetts Bay Transportation Authority (MBTA) controlled subway, trolley and bus services for Boston, but until the 1970s, passenger service to outlying communities remained in the hands of private companies. As brand new semi-trailers and coach buses hit the interstates, railroads across the country went into steady decline, especially on the East Coast.

The New York, New Haven and Hartford railroad had run freight trains to Franklin, Bellingham and Milford up until 1968, when the company folded (passenger service past Franklin had been discontinued in 1966). Its assets were acquired by Penn Central which was the only rail transit provider for the Franklin area by 1971. However, its future was in jeopardy. Fewer people traveled by rail than today, and Penn Central could hardly afford to run its trains any longer. The MBTA did its best to make sure that towns with rail access were able to maintain it, and applied pressure to Penn Central to keep up its services. Despite the pressure, officials in Boston and Franklin realized that it was only a matter of time before Penn Central went bankrupt. The end came in 1976, for Penn Central, which gave the MBTA enough time to buy up most of the rails between Franklin and South Station.

What was left of Penn Central joined the new federal company called Conrail (short for Consolidated Rail, a venture of bankrupt railroads). Conrail began running passenger trains to Franklin, and kept the rails in use until the MBTA took over the line entirely.

Meanwhile, the '70s were turning into a wild time at Franklin High. Construction of the new high school that opened in 1971 forced the high school to run double-sessions, with half of the students coming to class in the morning and the other half in the afternoon. With lax drinking laws, some students were showing up for afternoon class already drunk, or drinking beer in the parking lot. The administration tried hard to make friends with the students, inviting local bands to play on the fields. (Aerosmith played at FHS before they became top-ranked stars.)

Over at the Kennedy School on Pond Street, elementary school kids read an article about official state insects, and realized that Massachusetts did not have one. They hit on the ladybug as the perfect candidate, and petitioned Boston lawmakers to approve the idea. The legislature agreed to make the seven-spotted ladybug the official insect of Massachusetts, and invited the kids behind the idea to dress up as their favorite bug and visit the statehouse for a televised meeting with the governor.

Even with two new high schools (Tri-County was built in 1977), not everything was going well in the Franklin school system, as everyone in town found out when the teachers went on strike, but in 1976 such problems could be temporarily ignored as the town prepped for the national bicentennial followed two years later by the town bicentennial.

In 1970, the Historical Commission, a municipal body, was formed, supplementing the work of the earlier Historical Society, and started out by putting local memorabilia on permanent display in the library. Led by Herman Duvall, the new group decided to start a town museum in the South Franklin church after the Federated church granted it to the town in 1972. The Historical Commission launched an effort to create a National Register of Historic Places district, by listing dozens of historic buildings. Alice Vendetti went to work, and had a key role in creating the Dean College Historic District.

In the 'spirit of '76' a full length film about '76 festivities (for the national bicentennial) was put together by Delwyn Arnold and a team of volunteers. The 1978 town celebration was even larger—a number of time capsules were buried, and history teacher James Johnston released his first history of the town.

At the time of the town bicentennial, most people continued to work locally, and many companies pitched in to help with event preparation. The biggest employer was Garelick Farms, but many people also worked for Clark, Cutler, McDermott, Nu Style (a jewelry company), Electroformex Lab, Barnicle's macaroni plant, and others.

1978, the year of the town bicentennial, was also the year that nature dumped a record 54 inches of snow on town in the Blizzard of '78. Crawford and other DPW workers went to work from the start to clear roads paralyzed by snow. Driving a dump truck down Oak Street at nightfall, Crawford found himself following a four wheel drive vehicle. The car in front of him slammed on its brakes, coming to a stop, and then started up again going through the snow. Crawford's truck stalled in the snow. He had to spend a lonely night shoveling out his truck, and listening to the radio, hoping that the DPW would send along the Oshkosh all-weather truck to give him a tow. Robert Vallee kept measuring snow levels throughout the storm, and reporting them to Boston TV channels—it turned out that Franklin had some of the heaviest snow of any place in Massachusetts.

For 1979, the Italian community in Franklin planned to start celebrating the Feast of St. Rocco—a local tradition ever since.* It turns out St. Rocco is patron saint of many things, including bachelors, gravediggers, and diseased cattle. At early festivals, carnival favorites such as rides and fried dough were supplemented by beer and wine sales, but organizers banned alcohol after some carnival goers turned up inebriated.

The 1970s were a turbulent time in Franklin, but a time with some pretty memorable events.

* Until the '80s, Union Street's Italian neighborhood had centerline road paint in the colors of the Italian flag.

Chapter 20:

The Teachers Go on Strike

...One pregnant middle school teacher, who had struggled for years to have a child, miscarried after being remanded to the Framingham penitentiary...

Before she retired in 2012, Diane Poncz was one of only a handful of teachers at FHS who remembered the day when police officers hustled dozens of handcuffed teachers into 'paddy wagons' bound for the county jail in Dedham. If you find labor movements and strikes interesting, then look no further than Franklin for a dramatic story.

Besides a few minor disturbances in the mills at the turn of the 20th century, Franklin had witnessed very little sustained discontent or turmoil as a result of labor problems. By the late 1970s, the only rumblings of disquiet were coming from the teachers in the Franklin school system. There were mounting concerns about pay, seniority, and maternity leave

More significantly, teachers were getting concerned about rowdy, violent students. Members of the class of '78 streaked through the high school library—nude--on at least one occasion, and yearbooks from the '70s are filled with pictures of students fisting beers in the parking lot (the legal drinking age was 18 at the time). Brazen acts of violence against teachers, and even the police were common. One officer was clubbed on the head with a brick, while trying to break up a fight, and another was seriously injured when thrown off the rail bridge in the downtown by a gang. Franklin students had also trashed the common, leaving it covered in broken glass, and according to one legend, even tried to get the whole school 'high' by burning marijuana in the air vents.

Massachusetts, like most states forbids teachers and other government employees from going on strike. Legislators in Boston learned valuable lessons from the 1919 Boston police strike, during which lawlessness reigned in the city. They hoped never to have to deal with a public sector strike again, if it could be avoided, and implemented increasingly strict regulations. During the '60s and '70s, strikers elsewhere had had quite a lot of success with achieving their goals, a fact not lost on the powerful Massachusetts Teacher's Association--the statewide union for public school educators.

In September 1977, Franklin students returned from summer break, looking forward to another school year, while at the same time wishing that the summer could continue. To their surprise, it was not long until they were out of school on an indefinite break. Only a few days after Labor Day, Franklin teachers decided, overwhelmingly, to go on strike in violation of state law.

Today, the details of the early days of the strike--why it took place, and who instigated it--have become somewhat hazy. However, some former teachers claim that the Massachusetts Teacher's Association was applying quiet pressure, floating Franklin teachers up as a 'test balloon' to see how the state would respond.

Poncz had been hired as a Spanish teacher for the middle school only a few years earlier, in 1975. Fresh out of college, the Malden native had student-taught at Brookline High School before looking to the outer suburbs for a job. One of her colleagues from Brookline had moved to the Franklin school system, and recommended that she look into a job there. The first time Poncz traveled to Franklin, she drove straight through town and on into Wrentham before realizing that she had made a mistake--further proof of just how small our town was.

After graduating from high school, Poncz made the first of many trips to Spain. Back in the '70s, Spain was run by the dictator Francisco Franco, an old strongman. Franco's political enemies were often imprisoned and executed for opposing the regime. His opponents lived in constant expectation of a knock on the door at midnight. Poncz could hardly have guessed that only a few years after her trip to Spain, the police would be knocking on *her* door at midnight.

The strike involved every teacher to some degree. Many, including Poncz joined the strike not because of any deep conviction, but because they wanted to support their coworkers. Out of the 286 teachers in the school system, almost all participated in the strike. There were a few who stayed at work, but they constituted a tiny minority. Many of those who crossed the picket lines did so out of concerns for their students, believing that the well-being of students ought to come before their own concerns. In the years after the strike, there was plenty of animosity between the teachers who went on strike, and those who did not.

Striking teachers picketed and marched outside the schools, leaving schools virtually closed for weeks. For most of the month of September, schools were open, staffed with a few fulltime teachers and as many substitutes as the School Committee could find. For weeks, only 75 percent of students attended school, and even larger numbers turned up only for their homeroom classes, to be marked "here" in the roster. Parents were worried, choosing to keep their kids home rather than sending them to school. Adding to the sense of crisis, rumors and reports circulated amongst parents of teachers armed with baseball bats guarding the entrances to the schools.

If there were such militant strikers, they were in the minority. Regardless, the School Committee took a firm stance against the strikers, insisting that they return to work or face losing their jobs. The strikers ignored the warnings, and, egged on by the union, chose to continue the strike. The School Committee decided that enough was enough. Police officers and deputy sheriffs arrived at the high school and middle school, arresting 34 teachers in a single day.

Hauled off in police vans, the first batch of strikers appeared at court in Dedham where they were promptly sentenced to time in county jail. The Franklin School Committee and the Norfolk County courts hoped that a stern message had been sent to the strikers--call off the strike, or else. Even so, more than 150 full time teachers were *still* on strike. A week after the first 34 had gone to the 'slammer,' an astonishing 100 teachers were rounded up and arrested by the police. Appearing before Judge Greaney in Dedham, the teachers were fined 950 dollars each, and sentenced to jail for the roles they played. "I hope you don't confuse what you are doing with the great acts of civil disobedience that led to the creation of this country," Greaney said to the assembled teachers.

Poncz was one of the lucky ones. She had stayed with an elderly couple in Milford for her first year of teaching, but had moved to Boston a few weeks before the strike without informing her bosses. She was safe in Boston, where the police could not find her, but the elderly couple were very frightened when the police came knocking at their door at midnight, wanting to know where she was staying. Throughout the strike, she managed to avoid the mass arrests that netted so many other teachers.

The courts acted fast, sentencing the strikers in large groups of up to 30 at a time. Some teachers grinned defiantly while others wept uncontrollably as Greaney handed down indefinite sentences for contempt of court charges. The court had backed up the Franklin School Committee, ordering the teachers to return to work. Some Franklin teachers were sentenced to county jails, but others landed in state prisons. Female teachers ended up at the women's penitentiary in Framingham, while male teachers ended up sharing cells and meals with murderers and rapists. According to Judge Larry Parnell, who took part in sentencing, "We're putting them wherever there is floor space." The 14 female teachers sent to Framingham ended up staying in the prison hospital--there were no cells left any place else.

The remaining 180 teachers were told to end the 14 day strike, or they would all be rounded up and sentenced, per order of Judge Greaney. The School Committee offered its own solution, in the form of a new contract proposal. Meeting at the Franklin Country Club, only 3 teachers supported the new school contract. With nothing left to sacrifice, the jailed teachers voted over the telephone, rejecting the proposal. Despite their rejection of the proposal, Greaney stood firm with the county sheriff and local police to back him up. Realizing that they had lost, the remaining strikers agreed to negotiate an end the strike by October 1, 1977. Instrumental in this process was a man named Joe Ferrari, the long-time head of unionized teachers in Franklin. Meeting with school officials, Ferrari managed to ensure that all of the teachers involved would keep their jobs.

On October 1, the great Franklin teacher's strike came to an end. The teachers returned to work, bitterly in some cases, for very little had changed. Over the coming days, the teachers in county jail and state prisons were let out, but release was hardly satisfying. Franklin teachers had been defeated, sacrificed, some felt, in an experiment encouraged by the state union, and now the Franklin Education Association had to pay 150,000 dollars in fines. Additionally each teacher had to pay their own 950 dollar fine unless they wanted to go back to jail.

We can only wonder what would have happened if the strike had continued and all 180 teachers had been arrested. Prison officials had stated to reporters that there was no room left in the already overcrowded Massachusetts prison system to hold another 180 people. The county jails and state prisons were out of space, and there was no way that any of the town lock-ups could hold so many. Certainly Franklin's tiny police station would have been swamped by even a fraction of that number. Perhaps if the teachers had held out they would have won their protracted battle for improved contracts.

The experience left an indelible mark on all of participants, especially those who had been jailed. Some bore scars from their experiences in prison that would not heal for a long time. One pregnant middle school teacher, who had struggled for years to have a child, miscarried after being remanded to the Framingham penitentiary. She never returned to the Franklin school system.

One FHS art teacher (who ultimately headed the department), was one of the men sent to county jail. While cooped up in a cell, surrounded by criminals, he sketched elements of his bleak day to day life in prison. He brought these sketches with him when he left prison, and after his retirement many of the sketches ended up in the labor history collection of a Michigan university.

Today, it's hard not to sympathize with the striking teachers to some extent. Whether or not their decision to leave work and form a picket line was right or wrong is a matter of personal opinion. What is indisputable is the harshness of the government's response. Even though the teachers were in violation of the law, the police, the courts, and the Franklin School Committee seems to have been heavy handed in their application of justice and the restoration of order.

Looking back, it is also easy to understand why many parents were so angry. After all, the strike *did* impact students as well as teachers, and for years after the strike, the school system was in a state of civil war between the teachers who went on strike and those who did not. Many Irish American families from Boston had moved to Franklin in the '70s, attracted by the town's Catholic majority and parochial school. They also came to escape the violence and strife caused by busing between Boston's white and black majority neighborhoods. Like the busing crisis, the Franklin strike was characterized by excessive involvement of the courts and individual judges--Judge Garrity in Boston and Judge Greaney in Dedham.

When the strike came to an end, it sent a very clear message to other teachers across the country. Don't even think about it. Events in Franklin were widely reported across the country. Newspapers as far away as Texas and Florida carried detailed news of the crisis. In fact, even the *New York Times* carried news of the strike. Teachers' association magazines in states such as Missouri mentioned the event at different times, but since the 1970s, very little has been written about it. Here in Franklin, the teacher's strike is still murmured about in the school system. Some students have grandparents who went on strike, or parents who were in school at the time, but by and large the details have become hazy since the fateful September of 1977.

Chapter 21:

The 1980s

...Thanks in part to Swanbeck's new leadership, Franklin High was gaining a regional reputation as one of the best high schools in the state...

In the early '80s Franklin's public school system was in chaos. The much publicized teachers' strike of 1977 had left a deep divide within the school department.* One of the few, well organized departments at the high school was the foreign language department. FHS offered four different languages, in the early 1980s, including Spanish, French, Latin and Italian, and ran a number of foreign exchange programs.

Both Spanish and French exchange students lived with local families. After arriving in Franklin, French students were lectured on Franklin history by James Johnston. In 1985, the Spanish students arrived first, staying for two weeks, and leaving just in time for a batch of French students to arrive. The Spanish students visited Plimoth Plantation, the Prudential Center, the Kennedy Library, and Harvard University, skated at Veterans' Memorial Rink, and toured the Digital Equipment Corporation computer plant in Franklin (located on the old Sullivan dairy farm, the location considered for the Honeywell CPU factory in the early '70s). Toni Boix, a female student from Spain even spent her senior year of high school studying at FHS, experiencing snow for the first time in her life.

The exchange program was not one-sided. Franklin Spanish and French students alternated each year, taking either a trip to France or to Spain over February break.

For a while, foreign language was about the only thing that worked well at the high school. Too often, students were skipping class, camping out in the restrooms during class periods to smoke cigarettes. Non-smoking students and faculty often complained about the state of the restrooms, eye-watering dens of hazy blue gray tobacco smoke. Dorothy Swanbeck stepped in to fix things up.

Swanbeck was a 'townie,' born and raised in Franklin, where she lived in a stately house next to the common. She reentered college after the youngest of her five children entered kindergarten in 1968 and graduated summa cum laude from the University of Rhode Island, with

Low birth rates locally in the '70s led officials to close the Parmenter elementary school due to a lack of students.

a degree in English. Armed with her new knowledge in the field of teaching, she was appointed vice-principal of Franklin High School in 1977, two days before the teachers' strike began. By 1985, she had become the head of the Franklin Council on Drug and Alcohol Abuse, and was tapped to replace departing principal Dr. Maynard Suffredini.

On July 10, 1985, she was appointed principal of FHS.* Franklinites may not have realized it, but by appointing Swanbeck, they had turned over a new leaf.

Even before the start of 1985-'86 school year Swanbeck was involving herself in the school to a greater degree than any of her predecessors. At the beginning of August, she led a group of FHS students to a seminar at Waltham's Bentley College to hear First Lady Nancy Reagan speak about drug abuse prevention. Swanbeck made friends with teachers, students, and parents, and moved Franklin High in a new direction.

Students respected her—for example, after a metal railing in front of the high school was damaged, the Metalworking class repaired it and mounted a wreath on it, presenting it to her as a 1985 Christmas gift.

Under Principal Swanbeck, FHS turned itself around, and launched on a new course. Unlike some administrators, Swanbeck wanted to hear about her students' concerns. In the autumn of 1985, she launched the Principal's Breakfast, a monthly gathering of students picked at random through a lottery. Over breakfast, students were invited to voice any concerns no matter how trivial, for Swanbeck to hear and consider. Even more remarkable, Principal Swanbeck paid for the first breakfast out of her own pocket. One of the overwhelming concerns expressed by FHS students was the problem of smoking in the restrooms. Taking swift action, Swanbeck put in place stricter rules to punish students caught smoking in restrooms, eliminating the problem right away.

Thanks in part to Swanbeck's new leadership, Franklin High was gaining a regional reputation as one of the best high schools in the state. Franklinites had every reason to be proud. Not only was Franklin achieving great advances academically and in sports, but 22 members of Academic Decathlon team qualified for 1987 state championships. Franklin ended up competing successfully against communities such as Wayland.

Then again, there were some areas where Franklin simply outdid the competition. Physics students were treated to an unusual show by FHS teacher Ronald Defronzo, who lay down on a bed of nails with only a wooden board to protect his neck, as students smashed a cinder block
*Replacing Swanbeck as vice-principal was Dr. Kevin O'Malley.

that he was holding on his chest—a unique demonstration of physical principles to be sure.

Student involvement was taken to extremes by the Home Economics- Independent Living class, a program that sought to answer questions such as, "Can you make it on your own?"

In 1987, the Independent Living students staged a mock wedding, complete with wedding gowns, tuxedoes, and even a minister, brought in from St. John's Episcopal church. After the conclusion of the wedding ceremony, the bride and groom retreated to the Home Economics classrooms for a 'reception,' where the cooking students had baked a wedding cake.

Before the 1985-'86 school year came to a close, Franklin's population changed imperceptibly. Town Clerk Deborah Pellegri noticed a remarkable number while printing out population data from one of the town computers. Between the summer of 1985 and 1986, Franklin's population had grown from slightly more than 19,000 people to 20,000 residents. Bigger numbers were on the way.

Bringing sweeping changes to Franklin's small town existence, the construction of I-495 in 1965 helped to transform Franklin into commuter suburb and 'edge city' of today. The image shows the Route 140 interchange soon after its completion.

Constructed in the early '70s, Klein Innsbruck ski area in South Franklin catered to needs of downhill skiers in the Boston area during the decade's many energy crises. The ski area stayed in operation until 2000 and has since been converted into an over-55 community.

One of the characteristics of an edge city are the many shopping and entertainment locations outside of the traditional downtown. New shopping plazas such as the Horace Mann Plaza, seen being expanded around 1980, have drawn business away from downtown shops. Other plazas opened in the past 30 years include Village Plaza (1988), Stallbrook and Charles River (in Bellingham, built 1992 and 1998), and Big Y (2012).

Franklin tripled in population from only about 10,000 in 1960, to more than 30,000 in 2010. As new commuters moved in the '70s, '80s, and '90s, population grew faster than ever. Here, a police officer directs traffic on East Central Street sometime in the late '70s or early '80s.

Chapter 22:

The 1990s

...In the '70s, official assessments had offered rosy visions of a future Franklin with a hefty population of 70,000 by the early 21st century...

In 1990, Franklin was fast becoming what *Washington Post* journalist Joel Garreau called an edge city. The next year, bookstores around the country would stock his book, *Edge City: Life on the New Frontier*. What Garreau was witnessing around America was the development of so-called 'edge cities,' concentrations of office parks, warehouses, residential areas, and shopping plazas away from traditional urban areas. There is another description for the edge city phenomenon--urban sprawl.

Massachusetts has always been a densely populated state compared with California, Pennsylvania, and New York. Suburbs sprang up around Boston very early on. Amongst them were towns and cities such as Newton, Waltham, Framingham, Natick, and many others. For all the talk about the growth of the suburbs during the 1950s, the few new suburbs that grew up around Boston were still quite close to the city. Residents of Natick, Wayland, Lexington, Wellesley, and other sites of suburban growth had probably never heard of Franklin, unless they were fans of downhill skiing.

As these towns became suburbanized, other communities did their best to slow growth, limiting construction of new housing developments and apartment complexes and imposing more restrictive zoning. Communities such as Weston and Dover made it difficult for families to find housing in the Greater Boston area, putting strict limits on development. So, developers skipped those towns, and looked to towns further out, along the Massachusetts Turnpike and the new interstates such as I-495.

Franklin, Bellingham, Medway, Wrentham, and Plainville, all fit the bill. Each town had plenty of land available, some local industry, and small populations, as well as access to the newly constructed interstate. Starting in the late 1960s and early '70s, developers went to work in Franklin building the first neighborhoods for a new breed of commuter. Most of the early construction centered along Pond, Oak, King and Washington streets. Growth was slower than real estate agents might have wished, thanks to the gas crisis. Nonetheless, hundreds of ranch, split-level, and garrison-style colonial houses stand as a testament to a time when Franklin had just graduated from a small agricultural and manufacturing town.

By the 1980s, the housing market was picking back up again. Land was being bought up by voracious builders, foundations were being poured, and new neighborhoods were being built. Forge Park, a major new industrial park, was built after the state sold off part of the state forest. Elsewhere, the Charles River development off of Oak Street was built on land that had been agricultural up until the late '80s. Sometimes, new construction unearthed strange reminders of the Franklin's past. At one point, builders on Lincoln Street digging foundations for a new development discovered the remains of the Garelick brother's piggery. Even 20 or 25 feet down, the earth stank from years of accumulated pig feces.

In the '70s, official assessments had offered rosy visions of a future Franklin with a hefty population of 70,000 by the early 21st century. These goals were never realized because of changing demands of homebuyers. By the '90s, families had more money, and were more interested in buying larger homes on larger lots, than buyers in the '70s, ultimately limiting the size to which Franklin would grow.

During the autumn of 1990, and the winter of 1991, Franklinites of all ages were transfixed by the buildup for Operation Desert Storm in Saudi Arabia. As Franklin High's student newspaper, the *Panther Pause* reported in December 1990, more than 20 FHS graduates were taking part in the operation to free Kuwait.

Joseph Lynch, an FHS Latin teacher since 1988, tried to arrange an annual trip to Italy with his class to visit Roman ruins. Lynch was much liked by students both for his enthusiastic teaching style, and for his interesting field trips. Latin students took every opportunity to experience Roman and European culture, for example, taking the commuter rail to Boston's haymarket to learn about European street markets. In 1991, many students had signed up for the trip to Italy. Unfortunately, the trip ended in disaster. Because so many flights were being booked to carry soldiers to the Middle East, and because of concerns about terrorism, the trip was canceled. Many students lost money that they had invested.

In 1992 and '93, two bizarre, violent crimes rocked the community, leaving three people dead. At the very end of April, 1992, the Seguin family of Holliston left their children's soccer game. It was the last time that Mary Ann, and her two children were seen alive. Kenneth and Mary Ann Seguin were later described by a neighbor as an "all American" husband and wife with two children; Daniel, seven, and Amy, five years old. Mary Ann, a 34 year old Tupperware and Mary Kay saleswoman, was found floating face down in Sudbury River, wearing only a nightgown. Kenneth, a 35 year old marketing executive was found only a mile away, unconscious, and bleeding profusely from self-inflicted wounds.

What followed may have been one of the largest police searches in Massachusetts. Two hundred fifty state and local police officers combed the Sudbury River and Hopkinton Reservoir, equipped with wetsuits and scuba gear in search of the missing Seguin children.

Midway through the search, an anonymous caller telephoned State Police headquarters in Boston, and offered the police a location in Franklin to look. Searchers flew over in a helicopter, but couldn't make out anything suspicious. A few hours later, the same unidentified caller dialed the State Police again, elaborating on the previous directions. The police were left clueless as to the identity of the caller. Nevertheless, the caller's directions proved better than the ones that he or she had originally given police, and searchers turned their attention to Beaver Pond in Franklin.

At dawn the next morning, investigators from the Franklin Police, State Police, Middlesex County, and Norfolk County District Attorney's office turned up at Beaver Pond. It didn't take the police long to find the bodies of the two children, spaced about 25 feet apart, and three feet from the shore, in a marshy area away from the beach. Both children's throats had been cut.

The *Boston Globe* mentioned that, "Investigators were seen removing soil samples and searching the area [around the pond] with a metal detector, while divers waded through the pond." The Seguin children were taken to Worcester for autopsies. Meanwhile, Kenneth Seguin had been treated for his injuries and taken to Bridgewater State Hospital, for psychiatric evaluation. Seguin's lawyer insisted that his client was suicidal and suffering numerous gaps in his memory, but chillingly, a state psychologist found, "no major mental illness."

The multiple-murder shocked the Seguin family's Holliston neighbors even more than it did most people in Franklin. Special prayer meetings were held at the family's church, for neighbors and friends to remember them. Even more shocking, was the only suspect in the case-- Kenneth Seguin—father and husband. The solid case against him was strengthened with the discovery of his Dodge Spirit close to Hopkinton State Park. Blood stained clothes, and a knife that he had used in his attempted suicide were found on the seat.

As the investigation moved from the woods to the courtroom, prosecutors, friends, family, and bystanders wanted to know...why? Eleven days after the discovery of the bodies, the *Boston Globe* reported that Seguin had contemplated suicide a few months earlier, and that the family was having marital problems. Seguin claimed that his wife and children had been killed in a home invasion by two unidentified assailants, a claim dismissed by the police. As the investigation went on, new evidence against Seguin turned up--sleeping pills in his pick-up truck that were administered to his children, and blood stains on the underside of a mattress. The Seguins had shared a house with the Murphy family until only a few days before the murders, and the Murphys yielded testimony that indicated a souring marriage.

Police discovered Prozac pills, in the Seguin house during the investigation. Seguin's defense claimed that the medication might have turned him suicidal as well as violent, but other evidence pointed to a threat from his wife that she would leave him. The grisly murder left more questions than answers, questions that 16 jurors were forced to confront on a January day in 1993, as they traveled to the Seguin home, examined the suspect's automobile, and visited Beaver Pond.

Ironically, even as the jurors weighed the evidence, another murder was pending in Franklin. On a frigid winter evening, as snow fell from the sky, 42 year old letter carrier, Patrick Tyrell, arrived in Franklin aboard the commuter train from Boston. He worked long hours at the Central Square branch of the Cambridge Post Office, earning overtime pay to support his family. Disembarking in the middle of a snowstorm, Patrick called his wife Mary to tell her that he would walk home. The roads were too slippery to risk driving.

On the way home, Patrick got into a short altercation with a group of Franklin teenagers. Growing up in South Boston, Patrick was not afraid to fend for himself, and didn't take insults lying down. He should have walked away without a word, but instead, he told off the teenagers. Eighteen year old Stephen Daley responded by beating Patrick Tyrell to death with a baseball bat, leaving him by the side of the road. Daley was in police custody within hours, soon after charged with first-degree murder.

The two years that followed were difficult for Mary Tyrell and her two children. The family had moved to Franklin only a few years earlier looking for a safer place to raise their children. The family moved away from Franklin not long after the murder and the story took a strange twist from there. Mary took out a book of short stories to take her mind off of the ongoing Daley trial. Tucked inside the book was a 'Strike It Rich" ticket--a $20,000 winner. So began a new chapter for the Tyrell family. As Mary Tyrell told the *Boston Globe*, "I want to return it to whoever bought it...I'm not going to start being a thief at age 42."

After the Seguin and Tyrell murders, things in Franklin quieted down significantly, but occasional uproars and the endless flow of newcomers meant that the town was never truly sleepy anymore. Wolfgang Bauer, the town administrator, got flak for his handling in 1992 of the pollution problem at the former Nu Style plant. While it was in business, Nu Style had apparently run a clean operation, but after the company closed down in 1989, DPW workers chanced on a large amount of heavy metals and other pollutants while repairing a water main on Grove Street. The EPA got wind of the contamination, and launched a project to clean it up. Neighbors of the plant claimed that the DPW were late-comers, and that earlier reports of the pollution had been igonored.

In 1994, a new representative for Franklin and Medway walked through the doors of the State House to take office. James Vallee, a Franklin native, and 1984 FHS graduate already had an admirable track record before running for office, as a Democrat. A 1988 graduate of Providence College, Vallee became an attorney for Franklin-based law firm Cornetta, Ficco, Simmler & Vallee, while serving with distinction in the National Guard. Only 28 at the time of his election, Vallee contributed significantly to the town during his 18 years in office.

In the '90s new arrivals pouring into Franklin often brought young families, or couples planning to have children. The new arrivals were a different breed than many of the older residents of Franklin. They hailed from all over Massachusetts and the United States. Some came to stay, but many others were transient, living in Franklin for only a few years, before corporate transfers or job changes led them elsewhere. Although Franklin had many office parks, most of new families commuted elsewhere in Massachusetts.

As Franklin Public Schools strained under the weight of new students, it became clear that new schools would be needed. Already, the existing elementary schools had been expanded with the addition of temporary modular buildings to house offices and classrooms; but these were simply not enough. Compounding the problem, the largest school building in Franklin--the high school--was already too crowded to add any more classes. The high school building was shared by 9th-12th graders, 8th graders, and Oak Street elementary school.

The Town of Franklin started hunting for real estate. In 1996, the Dacey family put their former dairy farm on Lincoln Street up for sale, at an asking price of almost one and a half million dollars. Condominium builders looked the land over, but turned down the opportunity. The ground was swampy--too soft to build on. The Town of Franklin was more receptive, and in 1996, finalized a purchase of the Dacey property for more than a million dollars. The School Department hoped that a school might be built on the land, while the Fire Department hoped for a second fire station. Neither of the proposals were realized. After the land had been bought, the Town of Franklin realized that it was far too marshy to consider building on. The 100 acre tract was given over to build Dacey Field, but only a fraction of the land was used for the playground and sports fields. Dozens more acres were left unused, quickly overtaken by saplings.

On the other side of the town, a different property proved more promising. In 1996, the town opened the new Remington-Jefferson school to serve growing neighborhoods in South Franklin.

Even if a new fire station had been built on the Dacey property, it would have done little to prevent the tremendous damage caused by three large fires in 1995, 1996 and 1997. The first was a blaze that destroyed the old Thayer home on West Central Street (used by Dean College). Then, a blaze at Tri-County amounted to more one million dollars in damage. But the truly spectacular fire was one that engulfed the 127 year old Peirce Mansion on the Dean College grounds. The mansion, a dorm for 30 female students, caught fire in February, though, thankfully, no one was injured.

The '90s were high-paced, marked by rapid development and growth, expansion that would continue to increase in the 2000s. By the end of the decade, Franklinites were ready for whatever the 21st century might bring

Chapter 23:

Welcome to Edge City

...Clark, Cutler, McDermott, the company that began making horse blankets more than a hundred years ago, has been named one of GM's best and most reliable suppliers in recent years...

The 2000s were a time for Franklin to make sense of the all the growth that it had experienced since the 1970s. In 2000, the census revealed a population bigger than ever before—Franklin had outstripped towns like Milford and Attleboro in size.

Edge cities are known for their commuter culture, and Franklin fits the bill. Continuing a trend from the '80s and '90s, most Franklin residents now work much farther afield in jobs all across southern New England. Meanwhile, companies in Franklin employ people from other towns and other states such as Rhode Island. Today, companies run the gamut of industries—from medical device manufacturing to retail and shipping. Some of the biggest modern employers are the EMC Corporation, with a large presence at an office park off of King Street. Other large employers from the past are also going strong, such as Garelick Farms, although the milk for the processing plant now arrives by tanker, some from Vermont dairy farms close to the Canadian border.

The new schools and fire station planned in the '90s were finally completed. The Fire Department substation on King Street opened in 2000. A few years later, the new Keller-Sullivan school was opened along with the updated Oak Street-Horace Mann school. Sadly, the Red Brick school closed after 2000, for the first time in almost 170 years.

The town received an unexpected donation of land from local fishing enthusiast Ernest DelCarte, when he passed away in 2001. The property, worth three million dollars, was an old cranberry bog on Pleasant Street that DelCarte had flooded to create the Franklin Reservoirs. DelCarte opened a bait and tackle shop and allowed anglers to come in and use his ponds for fishing.

DelCarte's will had one restriction on the land—no fishing. Although he loved fishing, DelCarte hated the litter left behind by inconsiderate anglers. Only one person—one of DelCarte's lifelong friends—is allowed to fish the pond.

Early in the decade, the September 11, 2001 attacks took the entire country, by surprise. After the attacks, some FHS graduates joined the military, serving in Iraq and Afghanistan.

Shayne M. Cabino decided to serve his country by joining the US Marine Corps. While participating in the Iraq War, he was killed at the age of 19, in 2005. In the wake of Cabino's death, an annual motorcycle ride is held to commemorate the young marine, and the other young service members like him, who never made it home. His mother has gained national recognition for her work to end the wars in Iraq and Afghanistan.

Sergeant Robert Pirelli was also killed in Iraq while conducting combat operations on August 15, 2007. The 29 year old enlisted in 2003, becoming an airborne special operations infantryman, with numerous awards and decorations. A soldier intent on his mission, Pirelli learned to speak Arabic, preparing to communicate with local populations in Iraq.

These servicemen were commemorated at the end of the decade with a complete overhaul of the war monument on the common. The pillars with the names of those killed in combat during World War II, Vietnam, and other conflicts were rearranged, and a new monument was added for Iraq War casualties, and any casualties of the war in Afghanistan.

Defense contracts have helped some Franklin businesses such as Qinetiq, a company that designs and manufactures body armor for the military at its Forge Park plant. Other local manufacturers have seen tremendous success in unusual areas, such as Clark, Cutler, McDermott, a leading supplier of interior padding for GM, VW, and Russian car makers. Clark, Cutler, McDermott, the company that began making horse blankets more than a hundred years ago, has been named one of GM's best and most reliable suppliers in recent years. Remarkably, the factory on Fisher Street still uses many pieces of original manufacturing equipment dating back to the company's earliest days.

With a number of shopping plazas along West Central Street to lure shoppers away from the downtown, the Franklin Downtown Partnership tries to attract people back to small shops. Since the mid-2000s, the Downtown Partnership has sponsored many different events, including the Harvest Festival, the Strawberry Festival, and the farmer's market.

Another attraction in the downtown is the newly opened Franklin Historical Museum. After 2007, the town museum in the South Franklin church closed to the public, and in 2010 volunteers moved the museum's contents to the original town hall on West Central Street.

At the museum's opening ceremony, in May, 2010, Historical Commission Secretary Robert Percy, had a few things to say about the new museum:

"Just a few thoughts on this occasion; about six years ago, after a late historical meeting, I was giving Barbara Smith, our late, esteemed historian a ride home. We got talking, and she was describing an event in town history, and as was her style, the story was full of amazing details--names, addresses, visual descriptions--her knowledge of the town's past was encyclopedic...It was also daunting. She was not young and not in the best of health, and I knew she would not be with us forever. When there was a pause in the conversation, I think I said something like, 'That story you told was amazing. How will I; how are *we* going to be able to remember it?'"

"'Oh, you can't,' she said as though I were crazy. It suddenly made so much sense. We simply could not capture in written words, pictures, artifacts, [and] stories, everything there is to say and see about the town's collective memory. But this place, this museum, and everything in it is an attempt to do just that. When you think of it, everything is history. Everything that each of us does is history; part of a story, part of the overall picture of this town. We are so happy to offer this living museum to the public as a place where we can relive these stories, and share them with each other."

"It's appropriate that this building looks like a Greek temple. When it was built in 1842, many public buildings in our young and growing country were built in the Greek revival style, inspired partly by the new democracy in Greece and inspired partly by the ideals of Ancient Greece...This place is a temple to the collective memory of the town..."

"Some of these memories are already here, some are still waiting to be heard. This beautiful building can now serve as a meeting place where we can trade stories, laugh and remember..."

"Stanley Chilson was a resident of Franklin who took it upon himself to take videos and still photographs of the things that were happening in town: people watching baseball games, fighting fires, cleaning up trees after hurricanes...We invite you, the Stanley Chilsons of today, to share your talents with us and with the rest of the town so future residents of the town of Franklin get to know who we were and how we lived."

"This museum will be in constant motion. Return early and often and you will see things you hadn't seen on the previous occasion. We plan to rotate displays as we celebrate the contributions of veterans, women, farmers, kids, industrial workers, and tell their stories... or better yet, have them tell their own."

Chapter 24:

Recent Developments

...Current predictions peg Franklin's population at a stable 40,000 in the near future...

The 'Great Recession' that hit in 2009 has largely passed Franklin by. Most people have been able to keep their jobs, and the town is even planning for new development in the near future. Right now, planning is well underway for a new Franklin High School to replace the current 40 year old building. The new high school, based on the Whitman-Hanson model high school, is expected to be partly funded by the state, reducing the direct cost to the town, a project approved by voters on March 27, 2012.

Current predictions peg Franklin's population at a stable 40,000 in the near future. Growth has slowed down, now that virtually all available land in town is developed.

Franklin has come a long way—from Indian settlement to precinct to village to town, and now city.

THE END

Bibliography

• Blake, James Jr. Manuscript Map of Wrentham, Mass. October 1725. Massachusetts Historical Society.

• Blake, Mortimer. A History of the Town of Franklin, Mass.; From its Settlement to the Completion of its First Century, 2d March, 1878; with Genealogical Notices of its Earliest Families, Sketches of its Professional Men, and a Report of the Centennial Celebration. Franklin: Committee of the Town, 1879.

• Blake, Mortimer. Address delivered at the erection of a monument to the memory of the late Dr. Emmons at Franklin, June 17, 1846. Boston: Samuel N. Dickinson & Company, 1846.

• Chute, Rupert J.; Zanslaur, Thomas Lee. Dedication of the Newell Relic and Curio Hall. Providence: Snow & Farnham Company, 1909.

• Company History. Garelick Farms. http://www.garelickfarms.com/about/history.php.

• Comprehensive Water Pollution Abatement Plan; June 1971. Board of Public Works.

• Cook, Louis A., ed. History of Norfolk County Massachusetts: 1622-1918. New York; Chicago: S.J. Clarke Publishing Company, 1918

• Crawford, Santina & Howard. Personal interview. Nov. 10, Dec. 10, 2010.

• Diamond, Stephen Mark, Ph.D. From Township to Town: Franklin, Massachusetts between the Revolution and the Civil War. Cambridge: Harvard University Department of History[Thesis], 1976.

• Ellsworth, Lewis J., Secretary of the State Board of Agriculture. Massachusetts: Her Agricultural Resources Advantages and Opportunities. Commonwealth of Massachusetts, 1911.

• Fales, Bertha. A History of Norfolk. 1934.

• Fiore, Jordan D. Wrentham-1673-1973-A History. Wrentham: Town of Wrentham, 1973.

• Franklin Annual Town Report. Boston; Franklin: Sentinel Press, 1861-2010.*

• Franklin Federated Church-The Growing Church on the Common: History. Franklin Federated Church. 2010. http://www.franklinfederated.org/About_us_history.html.

• Franklin Fire Substation-Franklin, Massachusetts-Schematic Design- January 8, 1998. Carrell Group Architects.

• Franklin Sentinel. Franklin, Sentinel Press: 1878-1978.

• Franklin. Franklin Charter Commission. The Final Report of the Charter Commission of Franklin, Massachusetts. Franklin: Town of Franklin, 1978.

• Franklin's Civil War Page. John Leighton. Franklin High School. http://www.franklin.ma.us/auto/general/civilwar/.

• Goodwin, George M., Smith, Ellen, ed. The Jews of Rhode Island. Hanover: Brandeis University Press; University Press of New England, 2004.

• Hamilton, Duane Hurd, comp. History of Bristol County, Massachusetts, with Biographical Sketches of many of its Pioneers and Prominent Men. Philadelphia: J.W. Lewis & Company, 1883.

• Hamilton, Duane Hurd, comp. History of Norfolk County, Massachusetts, with Biographical Sketches of many of its Pioneers and Prominent Men. Philadelphia: J.W. Lewis & Company, 1884.

• Helen, Brunelle, and Jacques, Brunelle. The History of St. Mary's Parish on the Occasion of the 125th Anniversary: 1877-2002. 2003.

• Hewitt, Anne, and Shortt, Brian. The Franklin Country Club: 1899-1999. Franklin Country Club, Inc. 2000.

• History and Directory of Franklin, Mass. For 1890. Needham: A.E. Foss & Company, 1890.

• History of Franklin Paint Company. Franklin Paint Company. http://www.franklinpaint.com/index-9.html.

• History of Milford, Massachusetts: 1780-1980. Milford: Milford Historical Commission, 1980.

• Ide, Jacob, ed. The Works of Nathaniel Emmons, D.D.- Late Pastor of the Church in Franklin, Mass. With a Memoir of his Life. Boston: Crocker & Brewster, 1842.

• Jameson, E.O., ed. The History of Medway, Mass. - 1713-1885. Medway: Town of Medway, 1886.

• Johnston, James C., Jr. Franklin Almanac: 1995/96. Franklin: Franklin Almanac, 1995.

• Johnston, James C., Jr. Franklin. Dover: Arcadia Publishing, 1996.

• Johnston, James C., Jr. Odyssey in the Wilderness: The History of the Town of Franklin. Medway: The Wayside Press, 1978.

• Jones, Augustus F. A Franklin Album. Portland: Pilot Press, Incorporated, 1982.

• Jones, Augustus F. All About Dean. Portland: Pilot Press, Incorporated, 1976.

• Jones, Augustus F. Vignettes of Dean and Reflections. Portland: Pilot Press, 1978.

• Karr, Ronald Dale. Lost Railroads of New England: 2nd Edition. Peppperell: Branch Line Press, 1996.

• Kenney, Herbert A. Newspaper Row: Journalism in the Pre-Television Era. Chester: Globe Pequot Press, 1987.

• Lembo, Gail V. The Diaries of George M. Wadsworth: Volume Four- 1889 through 1893. 2002.

• Lembo, Gail V., comp. The Diaries of George M. Wadsworth: Volume One-1857 through 1863. 1998.

• Lembo, Gail V., comp. The Diaries of George M. Wadsworth: Volume Three- 1881, 1884 through 1888. 2000.

• Lembo, Gail V., comp. The Diaries of George M. Wadsworth: Volume Two- 1866 through 1871. 1999.

• Lockridge, Kenneth A. A New England Town: The First Hundred Years- Enlarged Edition. New York: W.W. Norton & Company, 1970, 1985.

• Maki, Thomas N. Men of Franklin- Franklin Citizens in the Kansas Free-State Conflict: Their Lives and Times. Hopedale; Franklin: Birch Hill Associates; Starburst Printing and Graphics, 1996.

• Nikolaidis, Nikolaos; Erkey, Can; Smets, Barth F., ed. Hazardous and Industrial Wastes: Proceedings of the Thirty-First Mid-Atlantic Industrial and Hazardous Waste Conference. Lancaster: Technomic Publishing Company, 1999.

• Our Temple. Temple Etz Chaim. 2010. http://www.temple-etzchaim.org/aboutus/history/.

• Packard, Harry A. "Farming in Massachusetts." Farm Journal February 1909. Print.

• Partridge, George F. History of the Town of Bellingham, Massachusetts-1719-1919. Bellingham: Town of Bellingham, 1919.

• Peters, John A.; Santoro, Nina C. A History of America's First Public Library at Franklin, Massachusetts: 1790-1990. Franklin Public Library Bicentennial Commission, 1990.

• Russell, Howard S. A Long, Deep Furrow: Three Centuries of Farming in New England. Hanover: University Press of New England, 1976.

• Spear, Robert J. The Great Gypsy Moth War: the history of the first campaign in Massachusetts to eradicate the gypsy moth, 1890-1901. The Maple-Vail Book Manufacturing Group, 2005.

• Staples, Barbara. The Bay State's Boston Post Canes: The History of a New England Tradition. Lynn: Flemming Press, 1997.

• Sullivan, Eugene. The Industrial History of Franklin. Franklin, 1928.—(See Sesquicentennial History)

• Taft, Ernest A. Bellingham. Charleston: Arcadia Publishing, 2003.

• The Bicentennial Anniversary of the Incorporation of the Town of Franklin Massachusetts: 1778-1978. Franklin, 1978.

• This is Franklin. Franklin Industrial Development Commission.

• Tommaso Juglaris: An Artist Between Europe and America. 2004.

• Tougias, Michael J. Outdoors in Franklin. Franklin: Town of Franklin, 2002.

• Wells, Frederick L. Early Norfolk Revisited: A Collection of Historic Photographs, Drawings, and Documents. Town of Norfolk, 1970.

• White, Kevin H. The Commonwealth of Massachusetts-Historical Data Relating to Counties, Cities and Towns in Massachusetts: Prepared by Kevin H. White Secretary of the Commonwealth. 1966.

• Wilder, Edward W. A Sanitary Survey of the Town of Franklin, Massachusetts. 1917.

• Wood, Frederick James. The Turnpikes of New England and Evolution of the Same Through England, Virginia, and Maryland. Boston: Marshall Jones Company, 1919.

*Note: Included within Annual Town Reports are the reports of companies and departments involved in providing municipal services in an official capacity, as well as annual School Committee reports. Different companies have printed annual reports over time, including Sentinel Press in Franklin, and many others in Boston. More recently, the reports have been issued by the town of Franklin without a collaborating publisher.

**All images included in this book are courtesy of the Franklin Historical Commission unless otherwise noted.

Index

About the Author

Eamon McCarthy Earls is a longtime resident of Franklin, and a graduate of Franklin High School, Class of 2012. *Franklin: From Puritan Precinct to 21st Century 'Edge City'* is his third book.

Starting out writing short stories, Eamon's interest in writing grew. Combining an interest in history with his writing, Eamon wrote two mystery novellas set in the 1920s and '30s, each inspired by family stories. The resulting book--*Kearns on the Double*--was published in 2009. The same year, and throughout 2010 Eamon began researching the Wachusett Reservoir in central Massachusetts, one of the main sources of water for the Greater Boston area. After uncovering an unexpected trove of information, he wrote the first complete history of the reservoir from its creation to the present, and published it in 2010 as *Wachusett: How Boston's 19th Century Quest for Water Changed Four Towns and a Way of Life*.

Eamon has been involved with the Franklin Historical Commission since 2010, and after the opening of the new Franklin Historical Museum on West Central Street, became interested in town history. Realizing the need for a new, updated history of Franklin, and building on his experience in writing and researching for *Wachusett*, he began looking into the town's past.

Made in the USA
Lexington, KY
11 November 2013